Du meine Seele, du mein Herz

50 Sololieder für feierliche Anlässe
von Hochzeit bis Trauer

50 Solo Songs for Special Occasions
from Weddings to Funerals

Mittlere bis tiefe Stimme und Orgel / Klavier
Medium-Low Voice and Organ / Piano

Herausgegeben von / Edited by
Roland Erben

C. F. PETERS

Ein Unternehmen der Edition Peters Group
FRANKFURT/M. · LEIPZIG · LONDON · NEW YORK

Begleitsätze zu allen Liedern als Audiofiles unter / Audio accompaniments for all the songs available from www.fabermusic.com/editionpetersresources

Cover Painting:
A Pathway in Monet's Garden, Giverny, 1902, Monet, Claude (1840–1926)
Österreichische Galerie Belvedere, Vienna, Austria / The Bridgeman Art Library

ISMN 979-0-014-11025-3

Vorwort

Die großen feierlichen Anlässe des Lebens – freudige wie traurige – werden nicht zuletzt durch ihre stimmungsvolle musikalische Ausgestaltung zu besonders bewegenden Ereignissen, die uns nachhaltig in Erinnerung bleiben.

Die vorliegende Ausgabe enthält die schönsten Sololieder für alle festlichen Gelegenheiten wie Taufe, Hochzeit und Hochzeitsjubiläen, Konfirmation und Kommunion, Gedenk- und Trauerfeiern. Auch zu außerfamiliären, zumeist „weltlichen" Anlässen – etwa Firmenjubiläen und Festakten – finden Interpreten und Veranstalter ein reichhaltiges Angebot für die Besetzung Singstimme und Orgel (oder Klavier).

Bei den 50 Liedern handelt es sich um Kompositionen, die nur selten speziell für solche Anlässe geschrieben wurden. Sie haben sich jedoch in langjähriger Praxis als bewährte Repertoirestücke etabliert. Ergänzend zu bekannten und häufig musizierten Titeln wurden auch einige weniger bekannte oder in dieser Form noch nicht erschienene Werke in die Sammlung aufgenommen.

Die Auswahl ist stilistisch vielfältig und reicht vom Barock bis zu einem Song aus dem Jahr 2004. Um einen internationalen Benutzerkreis anzusprechen, enthalten die meisten der deutschsprachigen Liedtexte auch eine singbare englische Übersetzung.

Es gehört zu den Eigentümlichkeiten mancher Kompositionen, dass sie für ganz unterschiedliche und bisweilen geradezu gegensätzliche Anlässe (wie Hochzeit *und* Trauerfall) gleichermaßen verwendbar sind. In Teil II der Sammlung sind solche Stücke zusammengestellt. Die anderen beiden Teile dagegen sind spezifischer ausgerichtet: Teil I auf freudig-festliche Familienanlässe wie Hochzeiten (einschließlich Silberner und Goldener Hochzeit etc.), Teil III auf Bestattungsfeierlichkeiten. Doch gibt es auch hier, wie die Praxis zeigt, immer wieder Repertoireüberschneidungen.

Um die Suche nach dem passenden Stück zu einem bestimmten Anlass zu erleichtern, werden Piktogramme für folgende fünf Kategorien verwendet:

 = Trauung (auch Silberne/Goldene Hochzeit etc.)

 = Taufe

 = Konfirmation, Kommunion, Firmung

 = Jubiläen und sonstige Festlichkeiten

 = Beerdigung, Totengedenken

Die Piktogramme finden sich im anlassbezogenen Verzeichnis (siehe übernächste Seite) und in den Anmerkungen zu jedem Lied im Anhang.

Da festliche Veranstaltungen oft im kirchlichen Rahmen stattfinden, wurde der Orgel als Begleitinstrument Priorität eingeräumt. Nicht selten haben schon die Komponisten selbst den Begleitsatz sowohl für Orgel als auch für Klavier ausgelegt (siehe z. B. Bruckner, Reger, Saint-Saëns). Für das Spiel auf der Orgel mit Pedal wurden vom Herausgeber die Angaben „Ped." und „Man." hinzugefügt.

Einige Stücke weisen im Original eine klaviertypische Begleitung auf (z. B. Schubert: *Ave Maria*); diese wurde für die Orgel adaptiert, zugunsten einer festlicheren Aufführung in kirchlichen Räumen. Die entsprechenden originalen Klaviersätze sind aber im Anhang zusätzlich wiedergegeben, wodurch für fast alle Stücke des Heftes eine Aufführung mit Klavier ermöglicht wird. Vielfach ist außerdem ein E-Piano einsetzbar, was weitere Optionen für eine Darbietung außerhalb des kirchlichen Bereiches eröffnet.

Bei einigen wenigen Stücken (z. B. von Grieg und d'Hardelot) erschien eine Orgeladaption nicht sinnvoll, in diesen Fällen wurde der originale Klavierpart beibehalten.

Die Sammlung ist vor allem auf zeitlose Kostbarkeiten hin ausgerichtet. Stücke aus der aktuellen Popularmusik, die oft kurzlebig sind, wurden daher nicht berücksichtigt. Jedoch ist das leichtere Genre durch die Evergreens *Amazing Grace* und *Because* sowie das als Filmmusik bekannt gewordene Lied *Lenas sång: Fly with me* vertreten.

Die vorliegende Ausgabe für mittlere bis tiefe Stimme enthält bis auf zwei Ausnahmen die gleichen Stücke wie der Band für hohe Stimme.[*)] Dabei wurden die Transpositionen so gewählt, dass die obere Grenze bei e^2/f^2 liegt und das fis^2 nur in wenigen Fällen verlangt wird. Dadurch sind die meisten Stücke nicht nur für semiprofessionelle, sondern auch für engagierte Amateur-Sängerinnen und Sänger erreichbar.

Mein Dank geht an die Sopranistin Elfriede Schramm (Oberursel/Taunus) und die Organisten Christoph Jakobi (St. Ingbert/Saarland) und Frank Hoffmann (Frankfurt/M.) für ihre beratende Mitarbeit.

Mögen die Kompositionen in dieser Sammlung einen erbaulichen und stimmungsvollen Beitrag zur Gestaltung vieler Festlichkeiten leisten.

Frankfurt am Main, im Mai 2013

Roland Erben

[*)] Die Ausgabe für hohe Stimme (EP 11202a) enthält zwei Sopran-Arien, die sich für eine Abwärts-Transposition nicht eignen, diese sind: J. S. Bach, *Mein gläubiges Herze* (Nr. 3) und Mozart, *Laudate Dominum* (Nr. 7). An deren Stellen treten im vorliegenden Band die originalen Mezzosopran- bzw. Alt-Arien *Bekennen will ich seinen Namen* von J. S. Bach und *Verdi prati, selve amene* von G. F. Händel.

Preface

That life's big ceremonial occasions – whether joyful or sorrowful – are so moving and make such a memorable impression is due in no small part to the music performed at them. This album contains a wide selection of solo songs for voice and piano (or organ) suitable for ceremonies such as baptisms, weddings and anniversaries, confirmations and first communions, memorial services and funerals. Many of the songs can also be used for formal, secular, occasions – for example, company anniversaries and celebrations.

Only a few of the 50 songs in this collection were specifically composed for such ceremonies but many have, over the years, earned their place in the standard repertoire. This collection also includes a number of less familiar songs, and works that have not before been published in their present form. The selection covers a wide range of styles, extending from the Baroque to the 21st century. Most of the German-language songs include English singing translations.

Many of the songs are equally well suited to performance at different and, in some cases, completely contrasting occasions (wedding *and* funerals, for example). Works of this kind are included in Part II of the collection. The other two sections have a more specific focus: Part I contains songs for joyful and festive family occasions such as weddings (including silver and golden wedding anniversaries etc.), while Part III is oriented towards memorial and funeral ceremonies. Even here, however, practice shows that there is frequently crossover between the categories.

In order to make it easier to search for a piece of music for a specific occasion, the following five symbols are used:

 = Wedding (also silver/golden anniversary etc.)

 = Baptism

 = Confirmation, first communion

 = Anniversary, jubilee and other festivities

 = Funeral, memorial service

The symbols can be found in the occasion-specific index (see right-hand page) as well as in the notes to the individual songs in the Appendix.

Because festive and ceremonial occasions often take place in a church context, priority has been given to the organ as accompanying instrument. It is not uncommon for composers to have arranged their accompaniment for both organ and piano (see, for example, the songs by Bruckner, Reger and Saint-Saëns). For the benefit of those playing an organ with pedal board, the editor has provided "Ped." and "Man." indications.

Some of the pieces originally had a particularly pianistic accompaniment (for example Schubert's *Ave Maria*). These have been arranged for organ in order to favour a more formal performance in a church. The original piano part has been included in the Appendix, meaning that any of the pieces in the volume can be performed on the piano. Of course, in venues which have neither organ or piano, an electronic piano can also be used.

In the case of a few of the works (those by Grieg and d'Hardelot, for example), an organ arrangement did not seem appropriate and the original piano part has therefore been retained.

The collection is oriented towards timeless classics and for that reason does not include recent popular songs. However, it does include the evergreens *Amazing Grace*, *Because* and *Lenas sång: Fly with me* (which reached a wide audience when it was used in the film 'As it was in Heaven').

With two exceptions, the present edition for medium to low voice contains the same pieces as the volume for high voice.*) These works have been transposed in such a way that e^2/f^2 represent the upper limit, with $f\sharp^2$ called for in just a few cases. As a result, most of the pieces are accessible not only to semi-professional singers but also to committed amateur singers.

I would like to express my gratitude to soprano Elfriede Schramm (Oberursel/Taunus, Germany) and to the organists Christoph Jakobi (St. Ingbert/Saarland) and Frank Hoffmann (Frankfurt) for their help and advice.

It is hoped that the works in this collection will make an uplifting and atmospheric contribution to numerous festive and ceremonial occasions.

Frankfurt am Main, May 2013

Roland Erben

(Translation: Richard George Elliott)

---

*) The edition for high voice (EP 11202a) contains two soprano arias that are unsuitable for transposing down. These are J. S. Bach's *Mein gläubiges Herze / My heart ever faithful* (no. 3) and Mozart's *Laudate Dominum* (no. 7). These pieces have been replaced in the present volume by the arias *Bekennen will ich seinen Namen* by J. S. Bach and *Verdi prati, selve amene* by G. F. Handel, originally for mezzo-soprano/alto.

Verzeichnis nach Anlässen / *Contents according to occasions*

Trauung / *Wedding*

Taufe / *Baptism*

Konfirmation, Kommunion, Firmung / *Confirmation, first communion*

Jubiläen und sonstige Festlichkeiten / *Anniversary, jubilee and other festivities*

Beerdigung, Totengedenken / *Funeral, memorial service*

INHALT / CONTENTS

Teil I Für freudige Anlässe (Hochzeit, Taufe, Jubiläum etc.)

Part I For Joyous Occasions (weddings, baptisms, anniversaries, etc.)

Teil II Für verschiedenste Anlässe

Part II For Various Occasions

Teil III Für Traueranlässe und Totengedenken
Part III For Mourning and Memorial Services

Appendix I: Klavierfassungen zu den Orgelbearbeitungen
Piano versions of the organ arrangements

Appendix II

Teil I
Für freudige Anlässe
(Hochzeit, Taufe, Jubiläum etc.)

Part I
For Joyous Occasions
(weddings, baptisms, anniversaries, etc.)

Für freudige Anlässe | For Joyous Occasions

1. *Bringt her dem Herren*

Bring to the Lord God

Heinrich Schütz (1585–1672)
SWV 283
Continuoaussetzung: Roland Erben

Gesang
Bringt her dem Her - ren, bringt her dem Her - ren, bringt her dem Her - ren, ihr Ge-wal - ti-
Bring to the Lord God, bring to the Lord God, bring to the Lord God, O all ye might - y
(Cont.)
Org. / Piano
(Man.)

3
- gen, bringt her dem Her - ren, bringt her dem Her - ren Eh - re und
men, Bring to the Lord God, bring to the Lord God glo - ry and

5
Stär - - ke, Eh - re und Stär - - ke.
hon - - our, glo - ry and hon - - our.

7
Al-le-lu-ja, Al-le-lu - ja, Al - le - lu - ja, Al-le-lu-ja, Al-le-lu - ja, Al - le - lu - ja,
Al-le-lu-ia, Al-le-lu - ia, Al - le - lu - ia, Al-le-lu-ia, Al-le-lu - ia, Al - le - lu - ia,
11
Al-le-lu-ja, Al-le-lu - ja, Al - le - lu - ja. Bringt her dem Her - ren, bringt her dem Her -
Al-le-lu-ia, Al-le-lu - ia, Al - le - lu - ia. Bring to the Lord God, bring to the Lord
15
-ren Eh-re sei-nes Na - - - - mens, be-tet an den Her - ren,
God all the glo - - ry of His Name. Wor-ship in His pres - ence,
19
be-tet an den Her - - - - - - - ren im hei - li-gen Schmuck.
wor-ship in His pres - - - - - - ence in ho - ly at - tire.

22
Al-le-lu-ja, Al-le - lu - ja, Al-le-lu - ja, Al-le-lu-ja, Al-le - lu - ja, Al-le-lu-
Al-le-lu-ia, Al-le - lu - ia, Al-le-lu - ia, Al-le-lu-ia, Al-le - lu - ia, Al-le-lu-
26
-ja, Al-le-lu-ja, Al-le - lu - ja, Al-le - lu - ja. Al-le
-ia, Al-le-lu-ia, Al-le - lu - ia, Al-le - lu - ia. Let all
29
Lan-de be-ten dich an und lob-sin - - - gen dir, lob-sin-gen,
na-tions wor-ship Thee now: Let them praise Thy Name; With sing-ing,
32
lob-sin-gen dei-nem Na - - men, lob-sin-gen, lob-
with sing-ing let them praise Thee, with sing-ing, with

34
-sin-gen dei-nem Na - men. Al-le-lu-ja, Al-le - lu - ja, Al-le-lu-
sing-ing let them praise Thee. Al-le-lu-ia, Al-le - lu - ia, Al-le-lu-
37
-ja, Al-le-lu-ja, Al-le - lu - ja, Al-le-lu - ja, Al-le-lu-ja, Al-le - lu - ja, Al-le - lu-
-ia, Al-le-lu-ia, Al-le - lu - ia, Al-le-lu - ia, Al-le-lu-ia, Al-le - lu - ia, Al-le - lu-
41
-ja, Al - le-lu - ja, Al - le-lu - ja,
-ia, Al - le-lu - ia, Al - le-lu - ia,
43
Al - le-lu - - ja, Al - le - lu - - ja.
Al - le-lu - - ia, Al - le - lu - - ia.
(ca. 4')

2. *Wachet auf, ruft uns die Stimme*

Sleepers Wake

J. S. Bach (1685–1750)
Kantate BWV 140
Arr.: Roland Erben

Org. / Piano
*)
piano
(Ped.)
4
forte
8
11
Zi - on hört die Wäch - ter
Zi - on hears the watch - man
piano
(Man.)
15
sin - gen, das Herz tut ihr__ vor Freu - den sprin -
sing - ing, and all her heart__ with joy is spring -

*) Kleine Noten nur bei Ausführung mit Klavier / *Notes in small print are intended only for performances with piano*

19
-gen, sie wa - chet, und steht ei - lend auf.
-ing. She wakes, she ris - es from her gloom;
forte
(Ped.)
23
piano
forte
27
30
tr
33
Ihr Freund kommt vom Him - mel präch - tig,
For her Lord comes down all - glo - rious,
(piano)
(Man.)
37
von Gna - den stark, von Wahr - heit mäch - tig,
The strong in grace, in truth vic - to - rious;
tr

41
ihr Licht wird hell, ihr Stern geht auf.
Her star is risen, her light is come!
forte
(Ped.)
44
47
tr
50
Nun komm', du wer - te Kron',
Ah! come, Thou bless - ed Lord,
(Man.)
53
Herr Je - su, Got - tes Sohn.
O Je - sus, Son of God,
Ho - si - an -
Hal - le - lu -
(Ped.)

57
- na!
- ia!
60
63
Wir fol - gen all' zum Freu - den - saal,
We en - ter glad the bri - dal hall
67
und hal - ten mit das A - bend - mahl.
and share with Thee the wed - ding feast.
71
(ca. 6')

3. Bekennen will ich seinen Namen

J. S. Bach (1685–1750)
BWV 200
Ed.: Roland Erben

9
Be - ken - nen will ich sei - nen
(tr)
11
Na - men, er ist der Herr, er ist der Christ, er ist der Herr, er ist der
13
Herr, er ist der Christ,
(tr)
15

17
in wel - chem al - ler Völ - ker Sa - men ge - seg - net
(tr)
19
und er - lö - set ist, ge - seg - - - - net und er - lö - set
(tr)
21
ist.
23

25
Kein Tod raubt mir die Zu - ver-
27
- sicht, der Herr ist mei-nes Le - bens Licht, der Herr ist mei-nes Le - bens
29
Licht, kein Tod raubt mir die Zu - ver - sicht, der Herr ist
31
mei - nes Le - bens Licht. Kein
(tr)

33
Tod raubt mir die Zu - ver - sicht, kein Tod raubt mir
35
die Zu - ver - sicht, der Herr ist mei - nes Le - - bens
37
Licht, der Herr ist mei - nes Le - - - - - -
39
- bens Licht, mei - nes Le - bens Licht, der Herr ist mei - nes Le - bens

41
Licht, der Herr ist mei-nes Le - bens Licht, der Herr ist
43
(tr)
mei - nes Le - bens Licht.
45
47
(tr)
(ca. 5')

4. *Schafe können sicher weiden*

Sheep May Safely Graze

J. S. Bach (1685–1750)
Kantate BWV 208
Arr.: Roland Erben

Org. / Piano

(Man.)

3

p *f* *p*

5

tr

Scha - fe_ kön - nen si - cher_ wei - den, wo_ ein_ gu - ter Hir - te_ wacht,
Sheep may_ safe - ly graze for ev - er,_ where a good_ shep - herd keeps his_ watch,

9

Scha - fe_ kön - nen si - cher wei - den,_ Scha - fe_ kön - nen_
sheep may_ safe - ly graze for_ ev - er,_ sheep may_ safe - ly,_

12

(tr)

si - cher_ wei - den, wo ein gu - ter_ Hir - te wacht, wo_ ein_
graze for_ ev - er, where a good_shepherd keeps his watch, where a good

16
gu - ter Hir - te wacht.
shep - herd keeps his watch.
19
p
f
p
21
tr
Wo die Lie - be wohl re - gie - ret, dort man Ruh und Frie - den spü - ret,
If there's love the food of liv - ing one can sense both peace and calm and
25
und was al - le glück - lich macht,
all that makes our land con - tent,
28
wo die
if there's
8va
(ad lib.)
p
f
p

31
Lie - be wohl re - gie - ret, dort man Ruh und Frie - den
love the food of liv - ing one can sense both peace and
34
spü - ret, Ruh und Frie - - - den, Ruh
calm, both peace and calm, both peace
37
und Frie - - den spü - ret, und was al - le glück-lich macht.
and calm, both peace and all that makes our land con - tent.
41
p
44
f
p
Scha - fe kön - nen si - cher wei - den,
Sheep may safe - ly graze for ev - er,
tr

47
wo— ein— gu - ter Hir - te— wacht, Scha - fe— kön - nen
where a good— shep - herd keeps his— watch, sheep may— safe - ly
50
si - cher— wei - den,— Scha - fe— kön - nen— si - cher— wei - den,—
graze for— ev - er,— sheep may— safe - ly,— graze for— ev - er,
53
(tr)
wo ein gu - ter— Hir - te wacht, wo— ein—
where a good— shepherd keeps his watch, where a good
56
gu - ter Hir - - te— wacht.
shep - herd keeps his— watch.
59
p
f
p
(ca. 5')

5. *He Shall Feed His Flock*

Er weidet seine Herde

Georg Friedrich Händel (1685–1759)
Messiah, HWV 56
Arr.: Roland Erben

Larghetto e piano

II (solo)
Org.*)
I
Ped.

4
He shall feed His flock like a shep - herd, and
Er wei - det sei - ne Her - de, ein gu - ter Hir - te, und
I

7
He shall ga - ther the lambs with His arm, with His arm,
sam - melt sei - ne Läm - mer in sei - nen Arm, in sei - nen Arm.
II

*) Klavierbegleitung: Anhang S. 150 / *Piano accompaniment; see Appendix, p. 150*

10
and car - ry___ them___ in His bos - om, and
Er nimmt sie mit Er - bar - men in sei - nen___ Schoß, und
I
13
gen - tly lead___ those___ that are___ with young;___ and gen - tly___ lead,___ and
lei - tet___ sanft,___ die ge - bä - ren soll,___ und lei - tet___ sanft,___ und
16
gen - tly lead___ those that are___ with young.
lei - tet sanft,___ die ge - bä - ren soll.
II

19
Come un - to Him all ye that la - bour, come
Kommt her zu ihm, die ihr müh - se - lig seid, kommt
I
22
un - to Him that are hea - vy la - den, and He will give you rest.
her zu ihm, mit Trau - rig - keit be - lad - ne, denn er ver - leiht euch Ruh.
25
Take His yoke up - on you, and learn of Him, for
Nehmt auf euch sein Joch und ler - net von ihm, denn
II
I

28
He is meek and low - ly of heart, and ye shall find rest, and
er ist sanft und de - muts - voll, dann fin - det ihr Ruh, für
31
ye shall find rest un - to your souls.
eu - er Herz, für eu - er Herz.
II
f
34
(ca. 5')

Für freudige Anlässe | For Joyous Occasions

6. *Where'er You Walk*

Georg Friedrich Händel (1685–1759)
Semele, HWV 58
Arr.: Roland Erben

Largo e pianissimo

Where-'er you walk, cool gales shall fan the glade,

Org. / Piano

(Ped.) (Man.)

4

trees, where you sit, shall crowd in-to a shade, trees, where you sit, shall crowd in-

7

-to a shade; where-'er you walk, cool

(Ped.) (Man.)

10

gales shall fan the glade, trees, where you sit, shall crowd in-to a shade,

13
(tr)
trees, where you sit, shall crowd_ in - to___ a shade.
17
(tr)
Where -'er you tread, the
f
p
(Ped.)
Fine
(ca. 4')
(Man.)
21
blush-ing flow'rs shall rise, and all things flour-ish, and all things flour-ish where-
24
Adagio
-'er you turn your eyes, where - 'er you turn your eyes, where -'er you turn your eyes.
Adagio
Da capo

7. Verdi prati, selve amene

Verdant Meadows, Groves Enchanting

Georg Friedrich Händel (1685–1759)
Alcina, HWV 34
Arr.: Roland Erben

Larghetta

Org. / Piano

5

10

(tr)

Ver - di__ pra - ti, sel - ve a -
Ver - dant__ mead - ows, groves en -

16

- me - ne, per - de - re - te la____ bel - tà.
- chant - ing, all your____ beau - ty will____ de - cay.

21
Ver - di___ pra - ti, sel - ve a - me - ne, per - de - re - te
Ver - dant mead - ows, groves en - chant - ing, all your___ beau - ty
27
la bel - tà. Va - ghi fior, cor - ren - ti ri - vi,
will de - cay. Love - ly flow'rs, swift flow - ing ri - vers,
33
la va - ghez - za, la bel - lez - za pre - sto in voi___ si_
Gra - cious smil - ing, heart be - gui - ling, Soon your charms___ will_
39
can - ge - rà. Ver - di___ pra - ti, sel - ve a - me - ne,
fade___ a - way! Ver - dant_ mead - ows, groves en - chant - ing,

45
per - de - re - te la bel - tà. E can - gia - to il
All your beau - ty will de - cay. To sad change the
51
va - go og - get - to all or - ror del pri - mo a - spet - to
fair scene's fa - ted, Like the earth when first cre - a - ted,
57
tut - to in voi ri - tor - ne - rà. Tut - to in voi
Yet 'twill all re - turn some day! Yet 'twill all
63
ri - tor - ne - rà. Ver - di pra - ti, sel - ve a -
re - turn some day! Ver - dant mead - ows, groves en -

68
- me - ne, per - de - re - te la bel - tà,
- chant - ing, All your beau - ty will de - cay,
73
(ritard.)
ad lib.
(a tempo)
per - de - re - te la bel - tà.
All your beau - ty will de - cay.
f
78
83
(tr)
(ca. 4')

8. *Caro mio ben*
Cavatina

Giuseppe Giordani (1751–1798)
Arr.: Roland Erben

Larghetto

p

Ca - ro mio

Org. / Piano

tr

p

(Ped.) (Man.)

6

ben, cre - di - mi al - men, sen - za di te lan - gui - sce il cor; ca - ro mio

f p

(Ped.) (Man.)

11

ben, sen - za di te lan - gui - sce il cor.

tr

f

tr

(Ped.)

15

Il tuo fe - del so - spi - ra o - gnor. Ces - sa cru - del tan - to ri -

(tr)

sim.

f

(Man.) (Ped.)

19
ad lib.
ad lib.
-gor; ces-sa cru-del, tan-to ri-gor, tan-to ri-gor. Ca-ro mio
sf
p
(Man.)
(Ped.)
(Man.)
23
tr
ben, cre-di-mi al-men, sen-za di te lan-gui-sce il cor, ca-ro mio
27
ad lib.
ad lib.
(tr)
ben, cre-di mi al-men, sen-za di te lan-gui-sce il
poco f
f
p
(Ped.)
31
cor.
f
p
f
tr
(Man.)
(Ped.)
(ca. 2')

9. *Die Ehre Gottes aus der Natur*

All Nature Sings God's Praises

Ludwig van Beethoven (1770–1827)
Op. 48 Nr. 4
Arr.: Roland Erben

Majestätisch und erhaben

Org.*)

Ped.

ff *mf*

Die Himmel rühmen des Ewigen Ehre, ihr Schall pflanzt seinen Namen fort. Ihn rühmt der Erdkreis, ihn preisen die Meere; vernimm, o Mensch, ihr göttlich Wort!

The boundless Heavens extol the Almighty, their thunder echoes forth His name. The earth exalts Him, the seas sing His praises, take heed, O man; their message hear!

6

p *mf* *p*

12

f *sf* *p*

*) Klavierbegleitung: Anhang S. 153 / *Piano accompaniment; see Appendix, p. 153*

19
Wer trägt der Him-mel un-zähl-ba-re Ster-ne?
What power rules o-ver thy con-stel-la-tions?
(sim.)
(Man.)
24
cresc.
Wer führt die Sonn' aus ih-rem Zelt?
Who guides the sun up there on high?
Sie kömmt und
Its rays smile
cresc.
p
cresc.
f
30
leuch-tet und lacht uns von fer-ne und läuft den Weg gleich als ein
down on the world, on all na-tions, tri-um-phant-ly it rides the
p
f
36
Held, und läuft den Weg gleich als ein Held.
sky, tri-um-phant-ly it rides the sky.
ff
(ca. 3')

10. *Ich liebe dich, so wie du mich*

I Love Thee As Thou Lovest Me

Ludwig van Beethoven (1770–1827)
WoO 123
Ed.: Roland Erben

Andante

Piano

Ich lie - be dich, so wie du mich, am A - bend und am Mor - gen. Noch
I love thee as thou lov - est me at ev - er noon and mor - row, there

5 war kein Tag, wo du und ich nicht teil - ten uns - re Sor - gen. Auch
was no day, on which not we did share our joy_ or sor - row; And

11 wa - ren sie für dich und mich ge - teilt leicht zu_ er - tra - gen. Du trös - te - test im
well it was for thee and me to_ go in all_ by_ shares,___ thou wouldst my rea - dy

16 Kum - mer mich, ich weint' in dei - ne Kla - gen, in dei - ne Kla - gen. Drum
com - fort be and_ I wept for thy ca - res, wept for thy ca - res. Then

p (sim.) mf p f f p dolce

Für freudige Anlässe | For Joyous Occasions

11. *Hear My Prayer / O for the Wings of a Dove*

Hör' mein Bitten / O könnt' ich fliegen wie Tauben dahin

Felix Mendelssohn Bartholdy (1809–1847)

Text: Psalm 55

Arr.: Roland Erben

Andante

Org. / Piano

p

Hear my pra - yer, O God, in-cline Thine
Hör' mein Bit - ten, Herr, nei - ge dich zu

5

ear! Thy-self from my pe - ti - tion do not hide; Hear my pra - yer, O God, in-cline Thine
mir, auf dei - nes Kin-des Stim - me ha - be Acht! Hör' mein Bit - ten, Herr, nei - ge dich zu

9

ear! Thy-self from my pe - ti - tion do not hide, Thy-self from my pe - ti - tion do not
mir, auf dei - nes Kin-des Stim - me ha - be Acht, auf dei - nes Kin-des Stim - me ha - be

13

sostenuto *pp*

hide. Hear my pra - yer, O God, in-cline Thine ear! Lord, hear me call, Lord, hear me call!
Acht! Hör' mein Bit - ten, Herr, nei - ge dich zu mir! Gott, hör' mein Flehn, Gott, hör' mein Flehn!

pp

*) Original: Viertelnote F (statt D), ebenso in T. 82 / *Original has crotchet (instead of D), also in bar 82*

*) Zur Kürzung kann nach Takt 47 sofort zu Takt 69 gesprungen werden (Weglassung des im Original für Chor gesetzten Teiles) /
If required, the following passage (originally scored for choir) can be omitted, so that bar 47 is followed by bar 69.

55
cresc.
sf
mf
-way would I rove, a - way would I rove, far a - way. In the wil - der-ness
Fein - de zu flieh'n, dem Fein - de zu flieh'n, weit hin - weg! Auf den Flü - geln
59
build me a nest, And re-main there for ev - er at rest, And re -
eilt' ich dann fort, fän-de Ru - he am schat - ti - gen Ort, fän - de
63
f
-main there for ev - er at rest, re - main there for ev - er at rest, re - main
Ru - he am schat - ti - gen Ort, hin - weg in die Fer - ne zu zieh'n, hin - weg
68
=de
p
3
cresc.
there for ev - er at rest. O for the wings, for the wings of a dove!
vor dem Fein - de zu flieh'n. O könnt' ich flie - gen wie Tau - ben da - hin,

72
p
Far a - way, far a - way would I rove! O___ for the wings,___ for the wings___ of a dove!
weit hin - weg in die Fer - ne zu zieh'n, O___ könnt' ich flie - gen wie Tau - ben da - hin,
76
cresc.
f
p
Far a - way, far a - way, far a - way, far a - way would I rove. In the
weit hin - weg, weit hin - weg, weit hin - weg vor dem Fein - de___ zu flieh'n. Auf den
80
cresc.
wil - der-ness build___ me a nest.___ And re - main___ there for ev - er at
Flü - geln eilt'___ ich dann fort,___ fän - de Ru - he am schat - ti - gen
83
f
dim.
p
rest.___ In the wil - der-ness build me, build me a nest,___ And re - main there for
Ort,___ auf den Flü - geln eilt' ich, eilt' ich dann fort,___ fän - de___ Ru - he am

87
f
ev - er at rest; In the wil-der-ness build me a nest, And re - main there for
schat - ti - gen Ort; Auf den Flü - geln eilt' ich dann fort, fän - de Ru - he am
91
cresc.
f
dim.
ev - er at rest, for ev - er at rest, for ev - - - - - er at
schat - ti - gen Ort, am schat - ti - gen Ort, am schat - - - - - ti - gen
p
96
rest. And re - main there for ev - er at rest, And re - main there for
Ort, fän - de Ru - he am schat - ti - gen Ort, fän - de Ru - he am
100
p
ev - - - er at rest.
schat - - - ti - gen Ort.
pp
(ca. 7' / 5' 30")

12. *Widmung*

Devotion

Robert Schumann (1810–1856)
Op. 25 Nr. 1
Text: Friedrich Rückert
Arr.: Roland Erben

Für freudige Anlässe | For Joyous Occasions

Allegretto con anima
Innig, lebhaft
Du mei-ne See - le, du mein
You are my soul and all my
Org. / Piano
mf
(Ped.)

3
Herz, du mei-ne Wonn', o du mein Schmerz, du mei-ne
heart, both bliss and woe to me thou art. You are my

6
Welt, in der ich le - be, mein Him - mel du, da - rein ich
world, where - in I'm liv - ing, my heav'n you are, in which I'm

*) T. 14 - 25 bei Ausführung mit Klavier: etc.
Bars 14 to 25 when played with piano:

21
-schie - den. Dass du mich liebst, macht mich mir wert, dein Blick hat
-pon me. That you love me, it gives me worth; I see my
24
ritard.
mich vor mir ver - klärt, du hebst mich lie - bend ü - ber
in - most self re - vealed. You lift me high be - yond my-
ritard.
p
(Man.)
27
ritardando
mich, mein gu - ter Geist, mein bess' - res Ich!
-self, my guard - ian an - gel, my bet - ter self!
ritardando
(Ped.)
30
f
Du mei-ne See - le, du mein Herz, du mei-ne Wonn', o du mein
You are my soul and all my heart, both bliss and woe to me thou
f

33
Schmerz, du mei-ne Welt, in der ich le - be, mein Him - mel
art. Oh you, my world where - in I'm liv - ing, my heav'n you
36
ritardando
du, da - rein ich schwe - be, mein gu - ter Geist, mein bess' - res
are, in which I'm giv - ing. My guard - ian an - gel, my bet - ter
ritardando
39
Ich!
self!
p
42
rit.
(ca. 3')

13. *Du Ring an meinem Finger*

Thou Ring Upon My Finger

Robert Schumann (1810–1856)
Op. 42 Nr. 4
Arr.: Roland Erben

Innig

p *con molto affetto*

Du Ring an mei - nem Fin - ger, mein gol - de - nes Rin - ge-
Thou ring up - on my fin - ger, My beau - ti - ful ring of

Org. / Piano

p

(Man.) *)

4

- lein, ich drü - cke dich fromm**) an die Lip - pen, dich
gold, My lips on thee fer - vent - ly lin - ger, And

7

fromm an die Lip - pen, an das Her - ze mein. Ich hatt' ihn aus - ge-
close the dear trea - sure to my heart I hold. My child - hood's dream had

p

(Ped.)

10

- träu - met, der Kind - heit fried - lich schö - nen Traum, ich
va - nish'd, A joy - ous dream se - rene and bright; A -

p

*) Bei Ausführung mit Klavier: LH mit Unteroktave spielen, wo möglich
If performed on a piano, add lower octave doublings to LH wherever possible

**) Anstatt „fromm" wird oft auch „fest" gesungen.
Singers often replace „fromm" by „fest".

13
fand al-lein mich, ver-lo-ren im ö-den un-end-li-chen Raum. Du
-lone I seem'd as if ba-nish'd to des-o-late re-gions of night. Thou
(Man.)
17
Ring an mei-nem Fin-ger, da hast du mich erst be-lehrt, hast
ring up-on my fin-ger, Hast giv'n to glad thoughts a birth, For-
21
mei-nem Blick er-schlos-sen des Le-bens un-end-li-chen, tie-fen Wert. Ich
-bid-dest clouds to lin-ger, Trans-form-est to rap-ture my life on earth, And
25
Nach und nach rascher / gradually faster
ritard.
will ihm die-nen, ihm le-ben, ihm an-ge-hö-ren ganz, hin
I'll live for him and near him; Will al-ways his re-main, To
Klavier / Piano:
etc.
ritard.
(Ped.)

(a tempo)
ritard.
sel - ber mich ge - ben und fin - den ver - klärt mich, und fin - den ver - klärt mich in
serve him, to bless and to cheer him; His glance of ap - pro - val to gain, his ap -
ritard.
(a tempo)
sei - nem Glanz. Du Ring an mei - nem Fin - ger, mein
- pro - val gain. Thou ring up - on my fin - ger, My
p
(Man.)
gol - de - nes Rin - ge - lein, ich drü - cke dich fest an die
beau - ti - ful ring of gold, My lips on thee fer - vent - ly
Lip - - pen, dich fromm an die Lip - pen, an das Her - ze mein.
lin - - ger, And close the dear trea - sure to my heart I hold!
(Ped.)
(ca. 3')

14. *Kavatine*

(Trauungsgesang / Wedding Song)

Louis Roessel (1828–1883)
Op. 25
Text: Paulus, 1. Korintherbrief
Arr.: Roland Erben

Ziemlich langsam

Org. / Piano

p (Ped.) (Man.)

1. Wenn ich mit Men-schen‿und mit En - gel - zun-gen
wenn ich Hab und Gut den Ar - men freu-dig

6

re - de-te und al - le Weis - heit hätt', und al - le Macht der Mäch - ti -
spen - de-te, und wenn ich mei - nen Leib dem Flam - - - men - to - de

11

- gen, und hät - te doch der Lie - be nicht, wär'
op - fer - te und hät - te doch der Lie - be nicht, es

mf *mf* (Ped.)

17

ich ein tö - nend Erz.
wär' ein ei - tel Tun.

1. 2. Und

22
2.
pp
(poco più mosso)
mf
3. Die Lie - be ist freund - lich, sie su - chet nicht das Ih - re, sie
2.
pp
(Man.)
27
mf
freu - et sich nicht der Un - ge - rech - tig - keit, sie freu - et sich der
mf
mf
(Ped.)
32
cresc.
Wahr - heit. Sie trä - get, sie glau - bet, sie hof - fet, sie dul - det
cre - - scen - - - do
37
(Tempo I)
Al - les. Die Lie - be
f
mf

42
hö - ret nim - mer auf, nein, sie hö - ret nie - mals

47
f etwas belebter
auf,
die Lie - be hö - ret nim - mer auf, sie hö - ret nie - mals
f
mf

52
p
ruhig
auf, nein, sie hö - ret nie - mals auf!
p
(ca. 4')

15. *Wo du hingehst*

Where'er Thou Goest

(Trauungsgesang / Wedding Song)

Eugen Hildach (1849–1924)
Op. 8
Text: Altes Testament, Buch Ruth
Ed.: Roland Erben

Lento, ma non troppo

dolce p (Man.) (Ped.) p

Org. / Piano

Wo du hin-gehst, da will auch ich, auch ich hin - ge - hen, und wo du bleibst, wo du bleibst, da blei - be ich auch, da blei - be ich auch! Wo du hin - gehst, da ge - he auch ich hin! Dein Volk ist mein Volk und

Wher - e'er thou go - est, I will go al - so, I will go al - so, and where thou lodg - est I will lodge, there I will lodge al - so, there I will lodge also! Where-e'er thou goest, there I will go al - so! Thy peo - ple, my people, and

2. Man.

poco a poco ritard.

Tempo I

17
f molto espr.
dein Gott ist mein Gott! Dein Gott ist mein Gott, ist mein Gott!
thy God is my God! Thy God is my God, is my God!
mf
mf
21
dolce
Wo du stirbst, da ster - be ich auch, und wo du ruhst, will ich be - gra - ben sein, und
Where thou diest, there I will die, where thou rest - est, there will I be buried, and
p
(Man.)
25
poco a poco ritard.
nur der Tod soll uns schei - - den! Wo du hin - gehst,
naught but death shall part us! Wher - e'er thou goest,
1. Man.
pp
poco a poco ritard.
29
da will auch ich hin - ge - hen!
there al - so I will go!
ritard.
(Ped.)
(ca. 2')

16. *Ich liebe dich*

I Love But Thee

Edvard Grieg (1843–1907)
Op. 5 Nr. 3
Text: Hans Chr. Andersen
Ed.: Roland Erben

Andante

Piano

p

Du mein Ge-dan-ke, du mein Sein und Wer-den! Du, mei-nes Her-zens ers - te Se - lig-keit!
You are my own, the ra-dience of my be - ing! You are my heart's de - sire, my on - ly joy!

pp *f*

Ich lie-be dich wie nichts auf die-ser Er - den, ich lie - be dich, ich lie - be dich, ich lie - be dich in Zeit und E-wig-keit, ich lie - be dich in Zeit und E-wig-keit!
I love you more than a - ny earth-ly trea - sure, I love but thee, I love but thee, I love you now and for e - ter - ni - ty, I love you now and for e - ter - ni - ty!

cresc. sempre *ff* *ritard.* *mp*

20
Ich den - ke dein, kann stets nur dei - ner den - ken, nur dei - nem
I think of thee in dream - ing and in wak - ing, thy per - fect
dim.
25
Glück ist die - ses Herz ge - weiht; wie Gott auch mag des Le - bens Schicksal
bliss I set all else be - fore; where ev - er fate my foot - steps may be
30
cresc. sempre
len - ken, ich lie - be dich, ich lie - be dich, ich lie - be dich in Zeit und E - wig - keit, ich
tak - ing, I love but thee, I love but thee, I love you now and for e - ter - ni - ty, I
35
ritard.
lie - be dich in Zeit und E - wig - keit!
love you now and for e - ter - ni - ty!
dim.

(ca. 2')

17. *Because*

Guy d'Hardelot (1858–1936)
Text: Edward Teschemacher
Ed.: Roland Erben

Poco adagio

Piano

f legato — *col* Ped. — *rit.* — *p*

5

Be - cause you come to me with naught save love And hold my hand, and lift mine eyes a - bove, A

9

wi - der world of hope and joy I see, Be - cause you come to me.

con tenerezza *poco rit.* *p* — *colla voce* — *poco rit.* — *mf*

13

p *ben legato* — *mf*

Be - cause you speak to me in accents sweet, I

rit. — *p dolce legato* — *cresc.*

17
più f
poco agitato
appassionato
find the ro - ses waking round my feet, And I am led through tears and joy to
cresc.
rit. colla voce
20
thee, Be - cause you speak to me.
cresc.
mf
ff
sostenuto
24
f maestoso
p con tenerezza
Be - cause God made thee mine I'll cherish thee, Through
sostenuto
ff
p
28
light and darkness, through all time to be, And pray His love may make our love di - vine, Be-
f
32
allargando
a tempo
- cause God made thee mine.
f
ff
colla voce
sempre
8va
8vb
(ca. 3')

18. *Entreat Me Not*
Wedding Song

Paul Dessau (1894–1979)
Ed.: Axel Bauni

Andante

Org. / Piano

p

(Man.)

En - treat me not to leave thee, and to re - turn from fol - low-ing af - ter thee;

6

11

for whith - er thou goest, I will go; and where thou

cresc.

p subito

17

lod - gest, I will lodge; thy peo-ple shall be

cantabile

p

22
my peo-ple, and thy God my God; where thou
più p
poco
p
28
di - est, will I die, and there will I be bu -
34
- ried; the Lord do so to me, and
39
more al - so, if ought but death part thee and me.
(ca. 3')

Für freudige Anlässe | For Joyous Occasions

19. *Wedding Song*

Whither Thou Goest
Wo du hingehst

Flor Peeters (1903–1986)
Op. 103c
Text: Old Testament, Ruth I: 16-17
Ed.: Walter E. Buszin

15
mf
there will I dwell. Whith-er thou go - - est, I will al - so
blei - be ich auch! Wo du hin - gehst, da ge - he auch ich
mf
20
allargando
go, whith - er thou go - est, I will al - so go.
hin, wo du hin - gehst, da ge - he auch ich hin!
allargando
25
f molto sostenuto e ben declamando
Thy peo - ple be my peo - ple, thy God be mine, thy
Dein Volk ist mein Volk, und dein Gott ist mein Gott, dein
molto sostenuto
f
(Man.)
30
allarg. ff
peo - ple be my peo - ple, and thy God mine!
Volk ist mein Volk, und dein Gott ist mein Gott!
allarg. ff
f
(Ped.)

36
poco meno sostenuto
p
Where thou di - - est, I too will die;
Wo du stirbst, da ster - be ich auch,
poco meno sostenuto
mf
p
(Man.)
41
and where they lay thee, there will I be lain; and nought but
und wo du ruhst, will ich be - gra - ben sein, und nur der
46
rall.
death shall part thee from me.
Tod soll uns schei - den!
rall.
52
poco animato
rall.
(Ped.)

57
Tempo primo
mf
Whith-er thou go - - est, there will I go al - so, and where thou
Wo du hin - gehst, da will auch ich hin - ge - hen, und wo du
mf
62
dwel - lest, there will I dwell. Whith-er thou go - - est,
bleibst, da blei - be ich auch! Wo du hin - gehst, da
mf
67
f
mf
I will al - so go, whith - er thou go - est, I will al - so
ge - he ich auch hin, wo du hin - gehst, wo du hin - gehst, da
f
mf
73
rall.
p
pp
molto rall.
go, will al - so go; with thee will I go.
ge - he auch ich hin, da ge - he ich hin.
rall.
molto rall.
p
pp
(ca. 3')

20. *Love's Philosophy*

Alan Hovhaness (1911–2000)
Op. 370
Text: Percy Bysshe Shelley

Andante (♩ ca. 76)

Org. / Piano

p

9

The fountains mingle with the river,

19

And the rivers with the ocean; The winds of heaven mix forever

27

With a sweet emotion; Nothing in the world is

37
sin - gle; All things by a law di - vine In one an -
45
- oth - er's be - ing min - gle: Why not I with thine?
53
See the moun-tains kiss high heav - en, And the waves clasp one an - oth -
62
- er; No sis - ter flow-er would be for - giv - en

69
If it dis - dained its broth - er;
And the sun - light clasps the

77
earth, And the moon - beams kiss the sea:
What are

84
allargando
all these kiss - ings worth, If thou kiss not me?

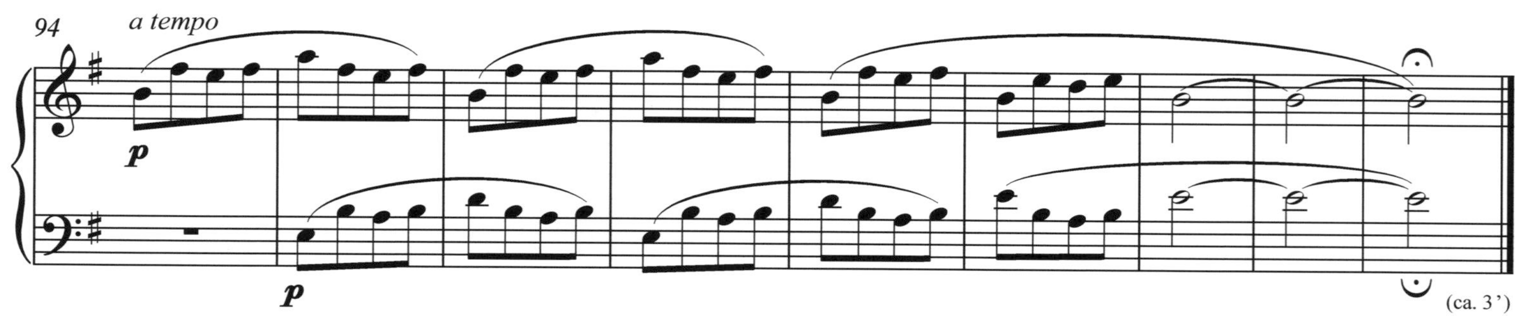
94
a tempo
p
p
(ca. 3')

21. *Fly With Me*

(Lenas sång)

Stefan Nilsson (b. 1955)
Text: Leyla Norgren

Piano / E-Piano

F — Csus4

Fly with me and take the sky

6

C — Dm — B♭ — F

Close your eyes, feel the wind. You and

12

Csus4 — C — Dm — Gm — C^7sus^4

I, we'll live to see When we reach the sky You will find.

18

C^{11} — F — B♭ — F — C — F

Fly a - way, take my hand, Spread your wings, reach the sky, I can make you be-

24
- lieve: Life is rich, rich with - in me. So fly a - way, hold my hand, Feel the
B♭ Gm C7sus4 C11 F B♭
29
wind, take the sky, Love will find, find a way, I be-lieve in
dm7 C/E F B♭ F
34
you. Fly with me, Fly with me. Night will fall,
Csus4 C B♭ F
40
stars will shine And the moon will smile to ease your mind.
Csus4 C Dm B♭

Für freudige Anlässe | For Joyous Occasions

66
sky. Love will find, find a way, I be-lieve in you, Fly with me,
C/E
F
B♭
F/C
Csus4
C
71
Fly with me.
B♭
3
3
F
C
76
Fly a-
Dm
Gm7
C
81
-way, take my hand, Spread your wings, reach the sky. I can make you be-lieve Life is
F
B♭
F
C
F
B♭

87
rich, rich with-in me. So fly a - way, hold my hand, Feel the wind, take the sky. Love will
Gm Csus4 C11 F B♭ Dm Dm7 C/E
93
find, find a way, I be-lieve in you, Fly with me, Fly with me,
F B♭ F/C Csus4 C B♭
99
Fly with me, Fly with me, Fly
F Fsus4 F Fsus4 F Gm7/F
mp
105
with me.
F Fsus4 F
p
(ca. 4')

Teil II
Für verschiedenste Anlässe

Part II
For Various Occasions

22. Jesus bleibet meine Freude

Jesu, Joy of Man's Desiring

J. S. Bach (1685–1750)
Kantate BWV 147
Arr.: Roland Erben

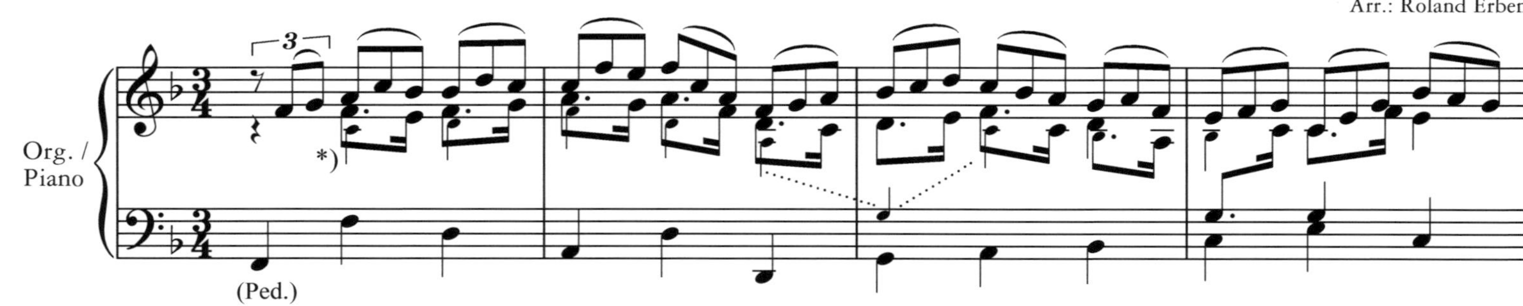

Org. /
Piano
*)
(Ped.)

5

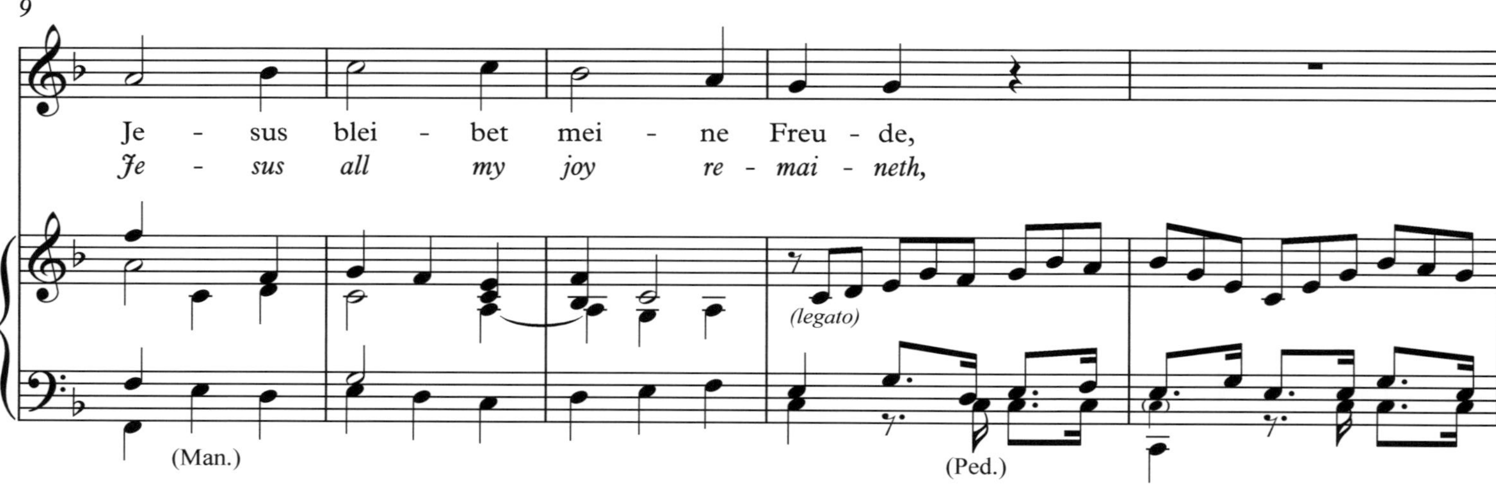

9
Je - sus blei - bet mei - ne Freu - de,
Je - sus all my joy re - mai - neth,
(legato)
(Man.)
(Ped.)

14
mei - nes Her - zens Trost und Saft,
my heart's so - lace and my stay.

*) Kleine Noten nur bei Ausführung mit Klavier. Bei Wiedergabe auf der Pedalorgel können die Mittelstimmen auf beide Hände aufgeteilt werden.
The small notes are intended only for performance on the piano. When playing on the pedal organ, the middle parts can be divided between the two hands.

18
22
Je - sus weh - ret al - lem
All my wounds to heal He
(Man.)
27
Lei - de, er ist mei - - nes
deig - neth, on Him all my
(Ped.)
31
Le - bens Kraft,
need I lay.
35

Für verschiedenste Anlässe | For Various Occasions

Für verschiedenste Anlässe | For Various Occasions

(ca. 4')

23. *Ave Maria*

Mélodie religieuse adaptée au 1er Prélude de J. S. Bach

Charles Gounod (1818–1893)
nach / *after:* J. S. Bach, Präludium BWV 846
Arr.: Roland Erben

Org. / Piano

p

Ped. Ped.: *sim. ad lib.*

3 *p* *pp*

A - - - - -

6

- ve Ma - ri - - - - - a,

9

gra - - ti - a ple - na, Do - - - mi - nus

cresc.

12

te - cum. Be - - - ne di - - - cta

pp *cresc.* *dim.*

Für verschiedenste Anlässe | For Various Occasions

30
cresc. molto
no - - bis, no - - - bis pec-ca - to - ri-bus,
ple - - na Do - - - mi-nus te - - cum,
cresc. - - - - - - - - - - - molto
33
nunc et in ho - - - - - ra, in
be - - - ne - di - cta tu et be - ne -
35
ho - - - ra mor - tis no - strae! A - - - - - -
- di - - - ctus fru - ctus ven - tris tu - i Je - sus.
dim.
38
rit.
- men! A - - - - - men!
rit.
p
pp
(ca. 3')

24. *Domine Deus*

Antonio Vivaldi (1678–1741)
Gloria (RV 589)
Continuoaussetzung: Roland Erben

(Largo)

Org. / Piano

(Man.)

3

5

8

Do - mi - ne De - us, Rex coe-le -

11

- stis, De - us Pa - ter, De - us Pa - - - - -

Für verschiedenste Anlässe | For Various Occasions

14
ter, o-mni-po-tens. Do-
17
mi-ne De-us, Rex coe-le-stis, De-us Pa-ter, De-us Pa-
20
ter, Pa-ter o-mni-po-tens.
23
Do-mi-ne De-us, Do-mi-ne
26
De-us, Rex coe-le-stis. De-us Pa-ter, De-us Pa-ter, Pa-

Für verschiedenste Anlässe | For Various Occasions

25. *Largo*

(*Ombra mai fù*)

Georg Friedrich Händel (1685–1759)
Xerxes, HWV 40
Arr.: Roland Erben

Larghetto

II. solo

Org.

Ped.

p *f*

8

p *f* (tr)

15

1. Om - - - bra mai fù di ve - ge -
2. (Tu) sei il mi - o ciel, te ne rin -

I II I

p

22

- ta - bi - le ca - ra ed a - ma - bi - le so - a - ve più, om - bra mai fù
- gra - zi - o non tro - vo spa - zi - o al - tro si bel. Tu sei il mi - o ciel,

Für verschiedenste Anlässe | For Various Occasions

29
di ve - ge - ta - bi - le ca - ra ed a - ma - bi - le so - a - ve più, ca -
te ne rin - gra - zi - o, non tro - vo spa - zi - o al - tro si bel. Te
35
- ra ed a - ma - bi - le, om - bra mai fù di ve - ge - ta - bi - le
ne rin - gra - zi - o, tu sei il mi - o ciel. Te ne rin - gra - zi - o,
41
ca - ra ed a - ma - bi - le so - a - ve più, so - a - ve più.
non tro - vo spa - zi - o al - tro si bel, al - tro si bel!
47
II
(tr)
2. Tu
(Fine)

26. *Bitten*

Gott, deine Güte reicht so weit
To Thee, My God

Ludwig van Beethoven (1770–1827)
Op. 48 Nr. 1
Text: Chr. F. Gellert
Arr.: Roland Erben

Feierlich und mit Andacht
Org. / Piano
p
(Man.)
cresc.

6
Gott, dei - ne Gü - te
To Thee, my God, whose
p

11
reicht so weit, so weit die Wol - ken ge - hen;
pres - ence fills the earth, and seas, and skies
cresc.
p

16
du krönst uns mit Barm - her - zig - keit und
To Thee, whose name, whose heart is Love, Will

Für verschiedenste Anlässe | For Various Occasions

Für verschiedenste Anlässe | For Various Occasions

27. *Ave Maria*

Ellens Gesang III / Hymne an die Jungfrau

Hymn to the Maiden

Franz Schubert (1797–1828)
D 839
Text: Sir Walter Scott
Arr.: Roland Erben

Sehr langsam
sempre simile
pp
Org.*)
Ped.

3
1. A - - ve Ma-ri - - - - a! Jung - - frau
1. A - - ve Ma-ri - - - - a, Mai - - den

5
mild, er - hö - re ei-ner Jung-frau Fle - hen, aus die - sem Fel-sen starr und
mild. Ah! lis - ten to a mai-den's pray - er, For Thou canst hear a - mid the
3
3

*) Klavierbegleitung: Anhang S. 155 / *Piano accompaniment; see Appendix, p. 155*

7
wild soll mein Ge-bet zu dir hin-we - - - hen. Wir
wild, 'Tis Thou, 'tis Thou canst save a-mid des-pair. We
9
schla-fen si-cher bis zum Mor-gen, ob Men-schen noch so grau-sam sind. O
slum-ber safe-ly till the mor-row, Though ba-nished, out-cast and re-viled: Oh
11
Jung-frau, sieh der Jung-frau Sor-gen, o Mut-ter, hör ein bit-tend Kind!
Maid-en, see a maid-en's sor-row, Oh Moth-er, hear a supp-liant child!
13
A - - ve Ma-ri - - - a!

15
2. A - - ve Ma-ri - - - -
2. A - - ve Ma-ri - - - -
17
-a! Rei - - ne_ Magd! Der Er - de_und der Luft Dä-
-a, Stain - - less_ styl'd! Each fiend of_ air or earth-ly
19
-mo - nen, von dei - nes Au-ges Huld ver-jagt, sie_ kön - nen hier nicht bei uns
es - sence, from this their won-ted haunt ex-il'd, Shall flee be-fore_Thy ho-ly
3
3
21
woh - - - - nen. Wir woll'n uns still dem Schick-sal beu-gen, da
pres - - - - ence. We bow be-neath our cares o'er-la-den, To

Für verschiedenste Anlässe | For Various Occasions

28. Gebet

Herr, den ich tief im Herzen trage
Be Near Me Still

Ferdinand Hiller (1811–1885)
Op. 46 Nr. 1
Text: Emanuel Geibel
Ed.: Roland Erben

26
f
dolce
Höch - ste wa - ge, sei Du mit mir, sei Du mit mir. O Du mein
heights, then guide me to do Thy will, Be near me still! Oh Thou my
f
decresc.
p
(Ped.)
(Man.)
33
f
mf
Trost, Du mei - ne Stär - ke, mein Son - nen - licht, bis an das
hope, my tow'r un - shak - en, My soul's true sun, Till earth's dark
mf
mf
40
f
En - de mei - ner Ta - ge sei Du mit mir, sei Du mit mir, bis an das
days shall be for - sak - en, Be near me still, be near me still! Till earth's dark
f
(Ped.)
47
En - de mei - ner Ta - ge sei Du mit mir, mit mir.
days shall be for - sak - en, Be near me, near me still!
dolce
(ca. 2')

29. *Panis angelicus*

César Franck (1822–1890)
Messe Op. 12
Arr.: Roland Erben

Poco lento
dolce, molto cantabile

Org. / Piano

p

(Ped.)

*)

6

cresc.

dim.

11

Pa - nis an - ge - li - cus

poco rall.

15

fit pa - nis ho - mi - num, Dat pa - nis coe - li - cus fi -

19

- gu - ris ter - mi - num: O res mi - ra - bi - lis

*) Gestrichelte Haltebögen und eingeklammerte Noten gelten vor allem bei Ausführung mit Orgel.
Dotted ties and notes in brackets are intended mainly for performance on the organ.

Für verschiedenste Anlässe | For Various Occasions

44
cresc.
-num: O - res mi - ra - bi - lis man - du - cat
48
f
Do - mi - num Pau - - per, pau - per ser -
51
dim.
- vus, et hu - mi - lis,
ff
Pau - - per,
dim.
cresc.
54
dim.
rall.
pau - per ser - - vus, ser - vus, et hu - - - mi -
rall.
57
- lis.
a tempo
p
rall.
pp
(ca. 3')

30. *Ave Maria*
(1882)

Anton Bruckner (1824–1896)
Ed.: Roland Erben

Alla breve. Weihevoll *)

p — *cresc. sempre*

A - ve Ma - ri - a, a - ve Ma - ri - a, gra - ti - a ple - na,

Org. / Piano

p — *sempre cresc.* — (Ped.)

7

gra - ti - a ple - na, **f** Do - mi - nus te - cum, Do - mi - nus *sanft / gently* te - cum: be - ne -

f — **p**

13

- di - cta tu in mu - li - e - ri - bus, *cresc.* et be - ne - di - *sempre cresc.* ctus,

cresc. — *sempre cresc.*

18

be - ne - di - ctus **fff** fru - ctus *decresc.* ven - tris tu - i, **p** Je - sus,

fff — *decresc.* — **p** — (Man.)

*) *With solemn mood*

25
mf
f
dim.
Je - - sus, Je - - - - - - - - - - sus.
mf
f
dim.
(Ped.)
32
p
pp
39
pp
cresc.
f
San - cta Ma - ri - a, Ma - ter De - i, o - ra pro no - bis,
pp
cresc.
f
45
dim.
pp
o - ra pro no - bis pec - - - - - ca - to - -
dim.
pp
(Man.)
50
ppp
cresc.
- - ri - bus, nunc et in ho - ra mor - - - tis
ppp
cresc.

Für verschiedenste Anlässe | For Various Occasions

31. *Deus Abraham*

Camille Saint-Saëns (1835–1921)
Arr. für Singstimme und Orgel: Roland Erben

Poco Adagio

p

De - us A - bra-ham, De - us I - sa-ac,

Org. / Piano

p

(Ped.)

5

et De-us Ja - cob vo-bis-cum sit: De - us A - braham, De - us I - sa-ac,

(Man.)

9

et De-us Ja - cob vo - bis-cum sit: Et ip - se con - jun - gat vos,

13

cresc.

Et ip - se con-jun-gat vos, im-ple-at - que be-ne-di-cti-o-nem su - am in vo - bis,

cresc.

mf

mf

17

p

be-ne-di-cti-o-nem su - am in vo - bis.

p

(Ped.)

Für verschiedenste Anlässe | For Various Occasions

21
Be-a - ti o - mnes qui ti - ment Do - minum, qui am - bu - lant in vi - is e - jus,
(Man.)
25
mf
be - a - ti o - mnes, be - a - ti o - mnes qui am - bu - lant in vi - is e - jus.
cresc.
29
sotto voce
De - us A - bra - ham, De - us I - sa - ac, et De - us Ja - cob vo - bis - cum sit:
sotto voce
(Ped.)
34
dolce
cresc.
f
et ip - se con - ju - gat vos, im - ple - at - que be - ne - di - cti - o - nem su - am in vo - bis,
dim.
38
dim.
rit.
p
pp
be - ne - di - cti - o - nem, be - ne - dic - ti - o - nem su - am in vo - bis. A - men.

(ca. 3')

32. Gott ist mein Hirte

The Lord is My Shepherd

Antonín Dvořák (1841–1904)
Op. 99, Nr. 4
Text: Altes Testament, Psalm 23
Arr.: Roland Erben

Andante
mp, quasi recit.
3
Gott, der Herr ist mein Hir - te, mir wird nichts man - geln,
God, the Lord is my shep - herd, I shall not want, shall
Org. / Piano
fp
lunga corona
pp
lunga corona

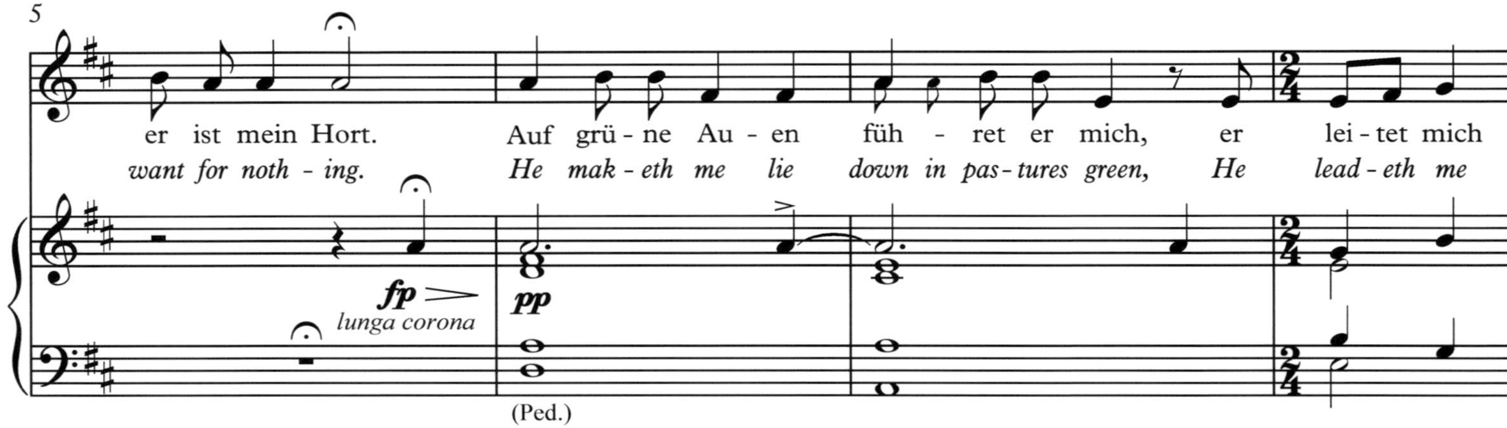
5
er ist mein Hort. Auf grü - ne Au - en füh - ret er mich, er lei - tet mich
want for noth - ing. He mak - eth me lie down in pas - tures green, He lead - eth me
fp
lunga corona
pp
(Ped.)

9
pp
mf
zu den stil - len, stil - len Seen. Mei - ner See -
where the qui - et wa - ters flow. He re - sto -
dim.
dim.
mf
(Man.)

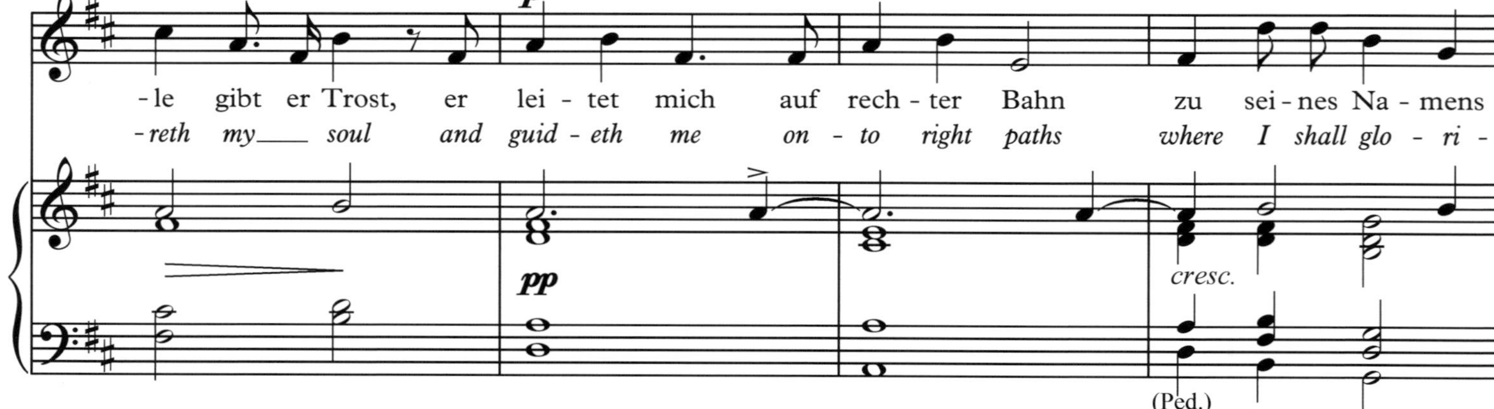
13
p
- le gibt er Trost, er lei - tet mich auf rech - ter Bahn zu sei - nes Na - mens
- reth my soul and guid - eth me on - to right paths where I shall glo - ri -
pp
cresc.
(Ped.)

Für verschiedenste Anlässe | For Various Occasions

Für verschiedenste Anlässe | For Various Occasions

33. *Cantique*

de Jean Racine

Gabriel Fauré (1845–1924)
Arr.: Roland Erben

*) Bei Ausführung mit Klavier in der LH die tiefe Oktave hinzufügen, wo möglich. / *When performing on the piano, add lower octave in the LH where possible.*

Für verschiedenste Anlässe | For Various Occasions

Für verschiedenste Anlässe | For Various Occasions

34
37
pp
40
dolce
Ré - pands sur
Ent - zünd' in
(+Ped.)
43
nous le feu de ta grâ - - ce puis - san - - te, Que
uns das Feu - er, das Feu - er dei - ner Gna - - de, durch
46
cresc.
f
tout l'en - - fer, que tout l'en - fer fuie au son
dei - ner Stim - me Macht ver - treib' die Höl - len -
cresc.
f

49
f
p subito
de ta voix, Dis - ci - - pe le som - meil d'une
-geis - - ter, die mat - te See - le neu durch
f
p subito
(Man.)
52
mf
â - me lan - guis - san - - te Qui la con -
dei - nen Geist er - la - - be, auf dass sie
mf
55
-duit à l'ou - bli, à l'ou - bli de tes lois.
nicht ver - gisst das Wort uns - res Herrn und Meis - ter,
(Ped.)
58
f
Qui la con - duit, à l'ou - bli, à l'ou - bli de tes
auf dass sie nicht ver - gisst das Wort, das Ge - setz, das von
f

61
p
lois! O Christ, sois fa - vo - rable à ce
Gott! Sei gnä - dig die - sem Volk und
p
sempre legato
(Man.)
64
peu - ple fi - dè - le; Pour te bé -
lass es dir ge - fal - len zu lo - ben
67
p
-nir main - te - nant ras - sem - blé, Re -
dich jetzt und al - le Zeit. Er -
(+Ped.)
70
cresc.
-çois les chants qu'il offre à ta gloire im - mor -
-hö - re die Ge - sän - ge, die dei - nem Ruhm er -
cresc.
73
f
decresc.
-tel - le. Et de tes dons qu'il re -
-schal - len, durch dei - nen Se - gen uns
f
decresc.

76
p
pp subito
-tour - - ne com - blé, et de tes
heim - - wärts ge - leit, durch dei - - nen
pp subito
(Man.)
79
pp
dons qu'il re - tour - - ne com - blé!
Se - - gen uns heim - - wärts ge - leit,
dolce
82
dolce
Et de tes
durch dei - - ne
85
(+Ped.)
pp
dons qu'il re -
Gnad', uns
pp
(Man.)
88
poco rall.
-tour - - - ne com - blé!
heim - - - wärts ge - leit!
ppp
(Ped.)
(ca. 5')
Für verschiedenste Anlässe | For Various Occasions

34. *The Lord's Prayer*

Flor Peeters (1903–1986)
Op. 102a
Ed.: Roland Erben

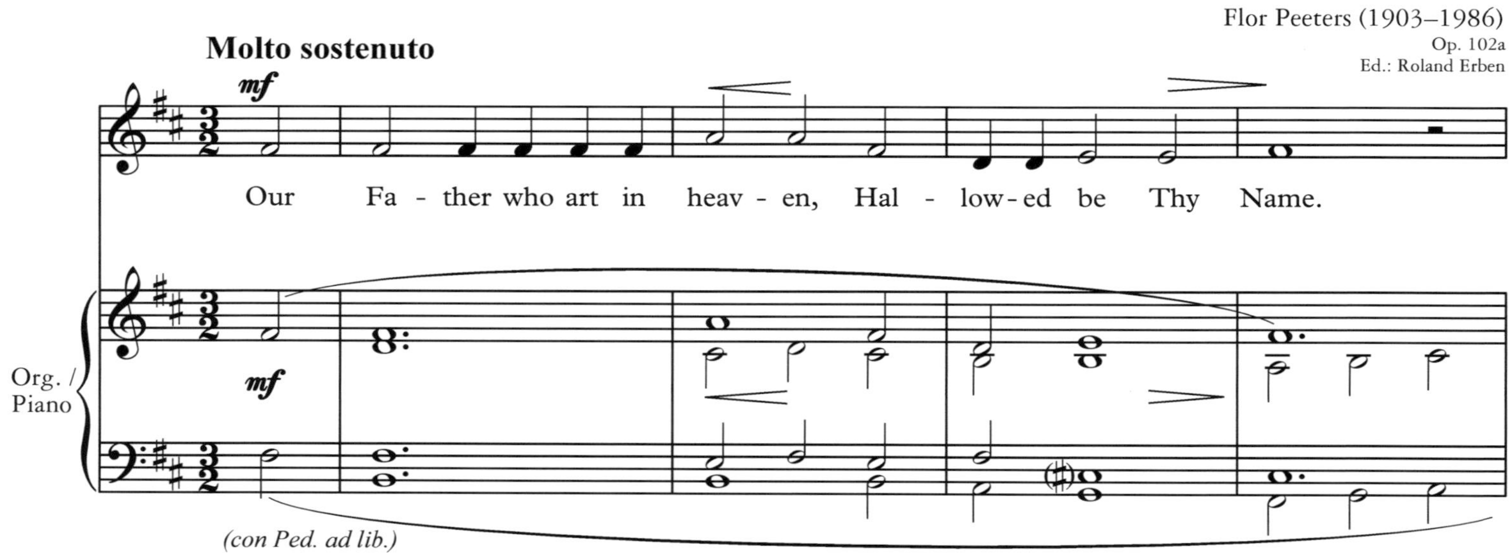

Molto sostenuto
mf
Our Fa - ther who art in heav - en, Hal - low-ed be Thy Name.
Org. / Piano
mf
(con Ped. ad lib.)

5
mf
p
Thy king - dom come, Thy will be done in earth, as it is in
mf
p

9
heav - en. Give us this day our dai - ly bread. And for - give us our

Für verschiedenste Anlässe | For Various Occasions

Für verschiedenste Anlässe | For Various Occasions

35. *The Call*

Ralph Vaughan Williams (1872–1958)
Text: George Herbert
Ed.: Roland Erben

*) Kleine Noten nur bei Ausführung mit Klavier / *Small notes only when played with piano*

17
Feast, as mends in length: Such a Strength, as makes his
A - tem al - ler Werk, de - nen Gna - de, Gna - - de nicht ge -
(Man.)
21
poco animato
f
guest. Come, my Joy, my Love, my Heart: Such a
- bricht, leh - re Lie - be, die be - kennt, Höch - ster,
poco animato
(m)f
(Ped.)
25
p
Joy, as none can move: Such a Love, as none can
der du al - le Lie - be bist, Sohn der Lie - be Je - su
p
29
rall.
Tempo primo tranquillo
pp
2
part: Such a Heart, as joys in love.
Christ, Sohn der Lie - be Je - - - - - su Christ!
2
2
pp
rall.
(Man.)
(ca. 2')

36. *Ave Maria*

Sur une « vocalise dorienne »

Jehan Alain (1911–1940)
Texte adapté par Albert Alain, 1942
Ed.: Roland Erben

Chant
Orgue
(Man.)

A - ve Ma - ri - a, gra - ti - a ple - na,

Do - mi - nus te - cum, be - ne - di - cta tu in

mu - li - e - ri - bus, et be - ne - di - ctus

fru - ctus ven - tris tu - i Je - sus. San - cta Ma - ri - a, Ma - ter De - i,

o - ra pro no - bis, o - ra pro no - bis

*) Zu diesem Stück und zur Aufführung siehe die Anmerkungen im Anhang / *For this piece and its performance see the remarks in the appendix*

Für verschiedenste Anlässe | For Various Occasions

*) Version nach J. Alains Autograph / *Version from J. Alain's autograph*

(ca. 3')

37. *When I Have Sung My Songs to You*

Ernest Charles (1895-1984)
Ed.: Roland Erben

Calmly (♩ = 80)

Piano

mp rit.

4 mf

When I have sung my songs to you, I'll sing no more. 'Twould be a sac-ri-lege

mf

8 ten.

to sing at an-oth-er door. We've worked so hard to hold our dreams,

espr.

12 agitato

Just you and I. I could not share them all a -

accel. - - - al - - - agitato

mf cresc.

Words and Music by Ernest Charles

Für verschiedenste Anlässe | For Various Occasions

Für verschiedenste Anlässe | For Various Occasions

38. *Amazing Grace*

American Folk Hymn
Text: John Newton (1725–1807)
Arr.: Roland Erben

Org. / Piano

1. A - maz - ing grace! How

(Ped.)

7

sweet the sound That saved a wretch like me! I once was

14

lost, but now am found, Was blind, but now I see. 2. T'was

21

grace that taught my heart to fear, And grace my

(Man.)

26
fears re - lieved. How pre - cious did that
31
grace ap - pear the hour I first be - lieved!
37
(Ped.)
3. The Lord has prom - ised
*) Yea, when this flesh and
**)
42
good to me; His word my hope se - cures;
heart shall fail, and mor - tal life shall cease,

*) Der kursiv gesetzte Text eignet sich für Trauerfeiern. / *Words in italics are suitable for funeral services.*

**) Frei imitierende Stimme: ad lib. als 4' auf gesondertem Manual; kann bei Ausführung mit Klavier eine Oktav höher gespielt werden (in der LH Basstöne ggf. weglassen). / *Freely imitating voice: ad lib. as 4' on separate manual. It may be played an octave higher when performed on a piano omitting the left-hand bass notes as necessary.*

47
He will my shield and por - tion be as long as
I shall pos - sess with - in the veil, a life of
(Man.)
(Ped.)
53
(with congregation ad lib.)
life en - dures.
4. A - maz - ing grace! How sweet the
joy and peace.
Through man - y dan - gers, toils, and
cresc.
f
59
sound That saved a wretch like me! I once was
snares I have al - read - y come; 'Tis grace has
65
poco rit.
lost, but now I found, Was blind, but now I see!
brought me safe thus far, And grace will lead me home.
poco rit.
ad lib.
(ca. 4')

Teil III
Für Traueranlässe und Totengedenken

Part III
For Mourning and Memorial Services

39. *Vergiss mein nicht*

Forget Me Not

J. S. Bach (1685–1750)
Schemelli-Gesangbuch, BWV 505
1. Str. (Continuoaussetzung): Eberhard Wenzel
2. Str. (Org. Arr.): Robert Franz

Aria *(Adagio)*

1. Ver - giss mein nicht, ver - giss mein nicht, mein al - ler - lieb - ster Gott.
1. For - get me not, for - get me not, O Thou Fa - ther and Lord!

Org. / Piano
(Cont.)
(Man.)

7
Ach, hö - re doch mein Fle - hen, ach, lass mir Gnad ge -
Hear, when in pray - er I bend me, O may Thy grace at -

12
- sche - hen, wenn ich hab Angst und Not; du mei - ne
- tend me, when I in an - guish call. O Thou, who

17
Zu - ver - sicht. Ver - giss mein nicht, ver - giss mein nicht.
lov - est all, For - get me not, for - get me not.

Für Traueranlässe | For Mourning

Für Traueranlässe | For Mourning

40. Schlummert ein, ihr matten Augen

Close Ye Now, Ye Weary Eyelids

J. S. Bach (1685–1750)
Aria aus: Klavierbuch der Anna Magdalena Bach
Begleitsatz und Continuoaussetzung (nach Kantate 82):
Roland Erben

Schlum - mert ein, ihr mat - ten Au - gen, fal - let sanft und
Close ye now, ye wea - ry eye - lids, soft - ly, calm - ly
Org. / Piano
piano
(Man.)

4
se - lig zu, schlum - mert ein, schlum - mert ein, schlum - mert ein, ihr
take thy rest, slum - ber on, slum - ber on, close ye now, ye
piano

8
mat - ten Au - gen, fal - let sanft und se - lig zu, schlum - -
wea - ry eye - lids, soft - ly, calm - ly take thy rest, slum - -

Für Traueranlässe | For Mourning

12
- - mert ein, ihr mat - ten_ Au - gen___ fal - let sanft und se - lig_ zu,___
- _ ber on, ye wea - ry_ eye - lids,___ soft - ly, calm - ly_ take_ thy_ rest,___
16
fal - - let_ sanft___ und se - lig_ zu.
soft - - ly_ rest___ on_ wea - ry_ eyes.
19
Welt, ich blei - be nicht mehr___ hier,_ hab ich doch_ kein Teil an_ dir,
World, with thee_ I would no lon - ger stay,_ far from thee_ I would a - way,
23
das_ der See - le könn - te tau - gen, das_ der See - le könn - te tau - gen; Welt, ich
care_ be - hind me, rest_ to find_ me, care_ be - hind me, rest to find___ me, world, with
tr

27
blei - be nicht mehr hier, hab ich doch kein Teil an dir, das der See - le könn - te
thee I would not stay, far from thee I would a - way, care be - hind me, rest to
30
tr
tau - gen. Schlum - mert ein,
find me. Slum - ber on,
34
schlum - mert ein, schlum - mert ein, schlum-mert ein, ihr
slum - ber on, slum - ber on, close ye now, ye
38
mat - ten Au - gen, fal - let sanft und se - lig zu, schlum - -
wea - ry eye - lids, soft - ly, calm - ly take thy rest, slum - -

Für Traueranlässe | For Mourning

*) Der im Original folgende Teil „Hier muss ich das Elend bauen" (18 Takte) wurde hier ersetzt durch das Nachspiel, das Bach diesem Satz in der Kantate Nr. 82 hinzugefügt hat. Diese Takte (hier 49 bis 57) können auch als Vorspiel vorangestellt werden, wobei die kleinen Noten in T. 57 dann mitzuspielen sind. / *The next section of the original, "Misery is here and wailing" (18 bars), has been replaced here by a postlude that Bach appended to this movement in Cantata 82. These bars (b. 49-57) may also be used as an introduction, in which the notes in small print in b. 57 should be played.*

41. *Bist du bei mir*

With Thou Beside

BWV 508 *)

Gottfried Heinrich Stölzel (1690–1749)
Continuoaussetzung: Roland Erben

Bist du bei mir, geh ich mit Freu - den zum Ster - ben_ und zu mei - ner
*With Thou be - side I tra - vel blest_____ to my_ ending and my fi - nal_*

Org. / Piano

7

Ruh, zum_____ Ster - ben und zu mei - ner Ruh. Bist du_ bei_ mir,
rest, my_____ end - ing and my fi - nal rest. With Thou be - side,

12

geh ich mit Freu - den zum Ster - ben_ und zu mei - ner_ Ruh, zum_____ Ster - ben und zu mei - ner
I tra - vel blest_____ to my_ ending and my fi - nal_ rest, my_____ end - ing and my fi - nal

tr

18

Ruh. Ach, wie ver - gnügt wär so mein En - de, es drück - ten_
rest. How pleased I'll be that Thou re - ceiv'st,_____ that Thou re -

*) Dieses Lied, das im zweiten Notenbuch der Anna Magdalena Bach von 1725 enthalten ist, wurde lange Zeit als Komposition von J. S. Bach angesehen.
This song included in the second Anna Magdalena's Notebook (1725) was long thought to have been composed by J. S. Bach.

Für Traueranlässe | For Mourning

42. *Ave verum Corpus*

Wolfgang Amadeus Mozart (1756–1791)
KV 618
Arr.: Roland Erben

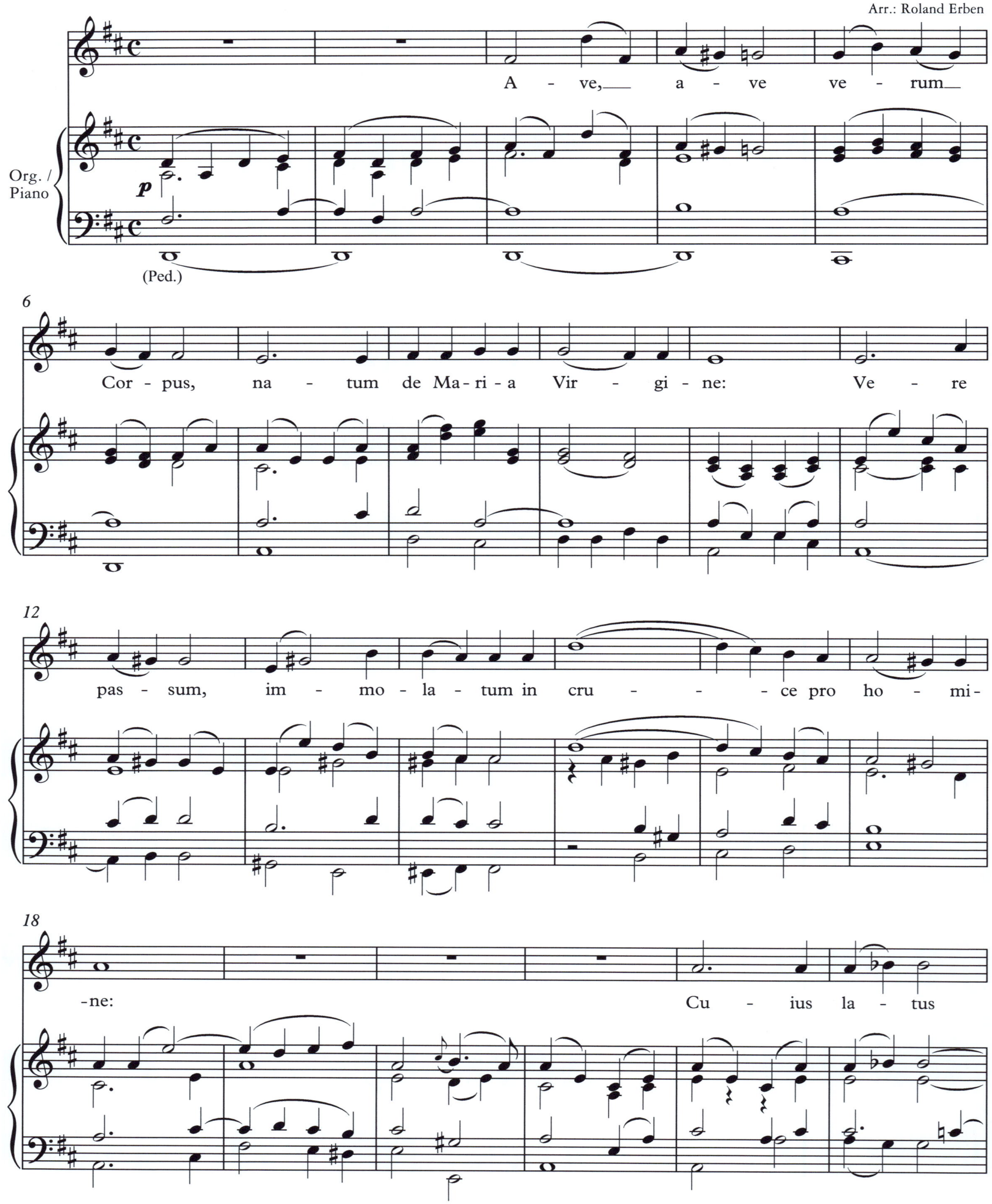

A - ve, a - ve ve - rum

Org. / Piano

p

(Ped.)

6

Cor - pus, na - tum de Ma-ri - a Vir - gi - ne: Ve - re

12

pas - sum, im - mo - la - tum in cru - - - ce pro ho - mi-

18

-ne: Cu - ius la - tus

Für Traueranlässe | For Mourning

43. *Im Abendrot*

Evening Glow

Franz Schubert (1797–1828)
D 799
Arr.: Roland Erben

Langsam, feierlich

I. solo

Org.*)

pp

Ped.

Oh, wie schön ist dei - ne Welt, Va - ter, wenn sie gol - den strah - let,

II I. solo

wenn dein Glanz her - nie - der - fällt, und den Staub mit Schim - mer ma - let,

II I. solo

wenn das Rot, das in der Wol - ke_ blinkt, in mein stil - les_ Fens - ter sinkt.

II *ppp* I. solo

*) Klavierbegleitung: Anhang S. 158 / *Piano accompaniment; see Appendix, p. 158*

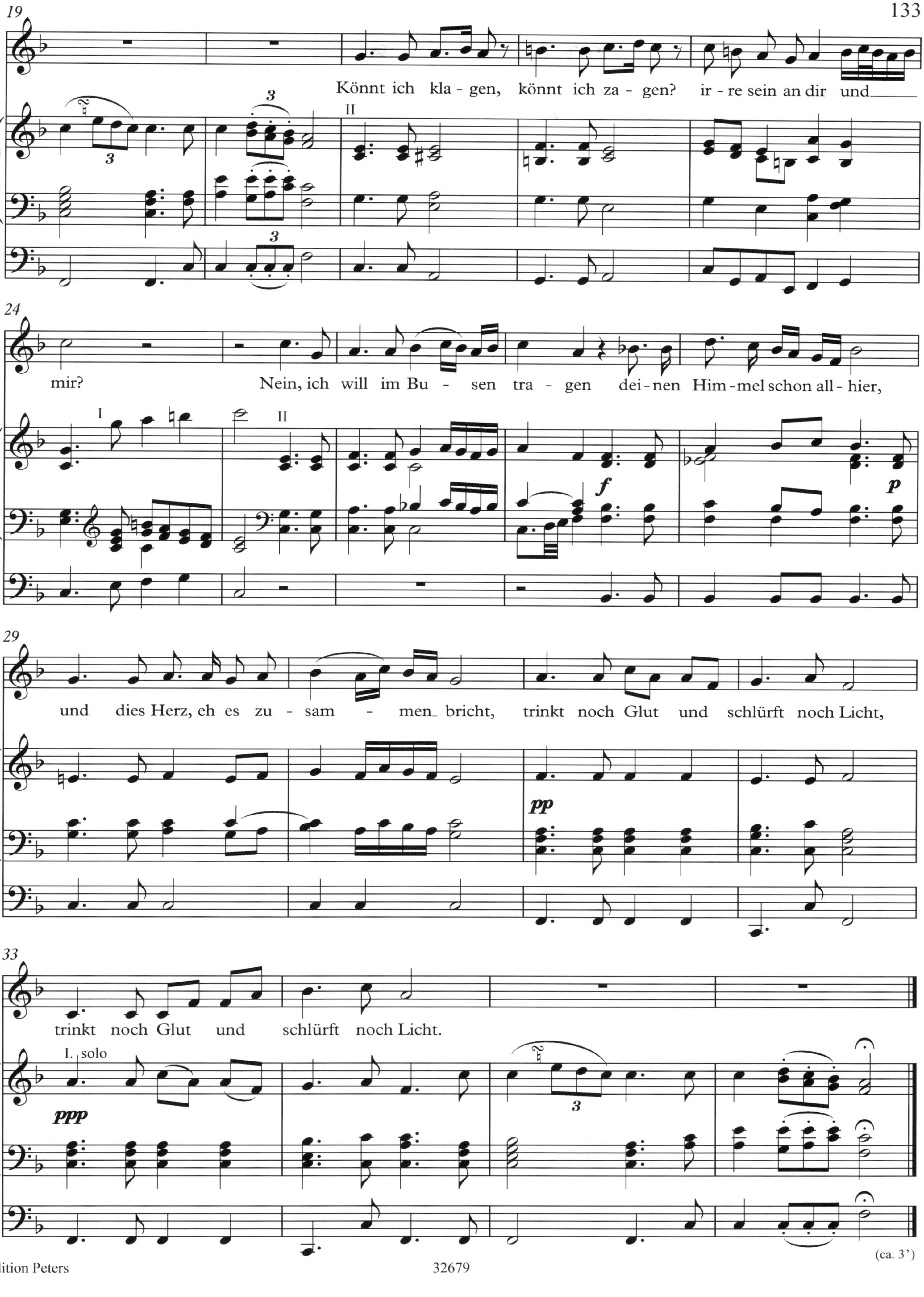

19
Könnt ich kla - gen, könnt ich za - gen? ir - re sein an dir und
3
II
3
24
mir? Nein, ich will im Bu - sen tra - gen dei - nen Him - mel schon all - hier,
I
II
f
p
29
und dies Herz, eh es zu - sam - men bricht, trinkt noch Glut und schlürft noch Licht,
pp
33
trinkt noch Glut und schlürft noch Licht.
I. solo
ppp
3
(ca. 3')

Für Traueranlässe | For Mourning

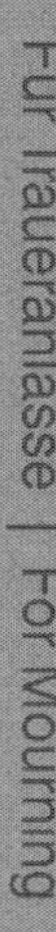

44. *Ins stille Land*

Franz Schubert (1797–1828)
D 403
Text: Johann G. v. Salis-Seewis
Ed.: Roland Erben

Mit Sehnsucht
1. Ins stil - le Land, wer
stil - le Land, zu
pp
Org. / Piano
(Man.)

6
lei - tet uns_ hin - ü - ber, ins stil - le Land, wer lei - tet uns_ hin-
euch, ihr frei - en Räu - me, ins stil - le Land, zu euch, ihr frei - en
cresc.

11
-ü - ber? Schon wölkt sich uns der A - bend-him - mel trü - ber, und
Räu - me für die Ver-ed - lung! zar - te Mor-gen - träu - me der

Für Traueranlässe | For Mourning

16
im - mer trüm - mer - vol - ler wird der Strand,
Wer
schö - nen See - len künft'-gen Da - seins - pfand.
Wer
cresc.
p
decresc.

21
lei - tet uns mit sanf - ter Hand hin - ü - ber, ach, hin - ü - ber ins stil - le
treu des Le - bens Kampf be - stand, trägt sei - ner Hoff - nung Kei - me ins stil - le
pp
cresc.

26
1.
2.
Land, ins stil - - le Land?
2. Ins
Land, ins stil - - le Land.
pp
dimin.
(ca. 3')

45. *Sei stille dem Herrn*

O Rest in the Lord

F. Mendelssohn Bartholdy (1809–1847)
Elias, Op. 70
Arr.: Roland Erben

Andantino

Sei stil - le dem Herrn und war - te auf ihn, der wird dir
O rest in the Lord, wait pa - tient - ly for Him, and He shall[…]

Org. / Piano

p

(Ped.)

4

ge - ben, was dein Herz wünscht, sei stil - le dem Herrn und war - te auf ihn, der wird dir[…]
give thee thy heart's de - sires:[…] O rest[…] in the Lord, wait pa tient - ly for Him and He[…] shall

(Man.) (Ped.)

8

ge - ben, was dein[…] Herz wünscht, der wird dir ge - ben, was dein Herz wünscht. Be - fiehl ihm dei - ne
give thee thy heart's de - sires,[…] and He shall give thee thy heart's[…] de - sires. Com - mit thy way un -

12

We - ge und hof - fe auf ihn, be - fiehl ihm dei - ne We - ge und hof - fe auf
- to Him, and trust in Him, com - mit thy way un - to Him, and trust in[…]

(Man.)

Für Traueranlässe | For Mourning

15
cresc.
ihn. Steh ab vom Zorn, und lass den Grimm. Sei stil - le dem
Him, and fret not thy - self be-cause of e - vil do - ers. O rest in the
cresc.
p
(Ped.)
(Man.)
18
Herrn und war - te auf ihn, war - te auf ihn. Sei stil - le dem Herrn und war - te auf
Lord, wait patient - ly for Him, wait patient - ly for Him. O rest in the Lord, wait patient - ly for
pp
(Ped.)
22
cresc.
ihn, der wird dir ge - ben, was dein Herz wünscht, der wird dir ge - ben, was dein Herz
Him, and He shall give thee thy heart's de - sires, and He shall give thee thy heart's de -
(Man.)
26
wünscht, der wird dir ge - ben, was dein Herz wünscht. Sei stil - le dem Herrn, sei stil - le dem
- sires, and He shall give thee thy heart's de - sires. O rest in the Lord, O rest in the
(Ped.)
30
Herrn und war - te, und war - te auf ihn.
Lord, and wait, wait pa - tient - ly for Him.
tr
(ca. 3')
Für Traueranlässe | For Mourning

46. *Ruhe sanft in Gottes Frieden*

Robert Schumann (1810–1856)
Nach / *after:* Op. 25 Nr. 26
Text: Th. Rehbaum (1835–1918)
Ed.: Roland Erben

Adagio

p

1. Ru- he sanft in Got - tes Frie - den, da voll - en - det dei - ne Zeit und dir sü - ße

Org. / Piano

p

(Man.)

6

Rast be - schie - den, Ruh und Rast nach Müh und Leid. Ist auch un - serm Blick ent - schwun - den,

(Ped.)

11

ritar - - - - - dando *(a tempo)* *p*

was von dir einst sterb - lich war, bleibt dein Bild doch al - le Stun - den uns im Her - zen

(Man.)

16

hell und klar.

(Ped.)

21
p
2. Wenn die Lie-ben von uns ge-hen, wenn ihr mü - des Au - ge bricht: ihr Ge-dächt-nis
p
(Man.)
26
bleibt be-ste-hen, es ver - geht_ und en - det nicht. Ru-he denn in stil - len Mau - ern
(Ped.)
31
ritar - - - - - dando
p
von des Le - bens Stür-men aus! Uns-re Lie - be, sie wird dau - ern ü - ber Tod und
p
(Man.)
36
Grab hin-aus.
(Ped.)
(ca. 2')

Für Traueranlässe | For Mourning

47. Selig sind des Himmels Erben

Blessed are the Heirs of Heaven

Wilhelm Berger (1861–1911)
Op. 49 Nr. II
Text: Friedrich Klopstock
Ed.: Roland Erben

Langsam

Org. / Piano

Se - lig, se - lig sind des Him-mels Er-ben, die To - ten, die im Her-ren ster - - - - ben, zur Auf - er - ste - hung ein - ge - weiht! In Frie - - den ru - hen sie, los von der Er - de Müh'. Ho-sian - na! Ho-

Bless - ed, bless - ed are the heirs of Hea-ven, the dead to whom the Lord hath giv - - - - en a pro - mised man-sion in the skies! A peace - - ful sleep is theirs, free from all earth - ly cares. Ho-san - na! Ho-

Für Traueranlässe | For Mourning

28
-sian - - na! Vor Got - tes Thron zu sei-nem Sohn be-
-san - - na! Be - fore the Throne, be-fore the Lamb, their
34
-glei-ten ih - re Wer-ke sie. Se - lig, se - lig
right-eous works shall fol - low them. Bless - ed, bless - ed
rit.
41
sind des Him-mels Er-ben, die To - ten, die im Her-ren ster - - - ben,
are the heirs of Hea-ven, the dead to whom the Lord hath giv - - - en
47
rit.
zur Auf - - er-ste-hung ein-ge-weiht!
a pro - - mised man-sion in the skies.
rit.
rit.
(ca. 3')
Für Traueranlässe | For Mourning

48. *Bitte um einen seligen Tod*

Prayer for a Blessed Death

Max Reger (1873–1916)
Op. 137 Nr. 1
Text: Nikolaus Herman (d. 1561)
Ed.: Roland Erben

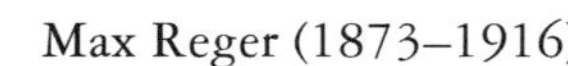

Ziemlich langsam
p
più p
1. Wenn mein Stünd - lein für - han - den ist, und soll hin - fahrn mein'
1. When at last comes my life's last hour, And death's road lies be -
Org. / Piano
(con Ped.)

4
pp
mp
Stra - ße, so g'leit du mich, Herr Je - su Christ, mit Hilf mich nicht ver -
- fore me; Lord Je - sus Christ, lend me Thy pow'r, To guide me and re -

8
p
pp
mp
- las - se, mein Seel' an mei - nem letz - ten End be - fehl ich dir in dei - ne Händ', du
- store me; When I go forth to that dark land I give my - self in - to Thy hand; Thou

Für Traueranlässe | For Mourning

13
rit.
pp
p
più p
wollst sie mir be - wah - ren. 2. Mein Sünd' mich wer-den krän-ken sehr, mein
shalt pre-serve my spir - it. 2. All my sins then will trou-ble me; My
18
pp
mp
G'wis-sen wird mich na - gen, denn ihr'r sind viel wie Sand am Meer, doch
con - science will op - press me; My sins a - bound like sands of the sea, But
22
will ich nicht ver - za - gen, ge - den-ken will ich an dein' Tod, Herr
let them not dis - tress me. Thy pre-cious death and blood so red, Lord
26
ppp
Je - su, und dein Wun-den rot, die wer-den mich er - hal - ten.
Je - sus, that for us was shed, Shall guard me and up - hold me.
(ca. 2')
Für Traueranlässe | For Mourning

49. *Pie Jesu*

Gabriel Fauré (1845–1924)
Requiem, Op. 48
Arr.: Roland Erben

Adagio (♩ = 44) *dolce tranquillo*

dolce

p

Org. / Piano

(Man.)

Pi - e Je - su Do - mi - ne, do - na_ e - is re - qui - em,

6

do - na_ e - is re - qui - em.

(Ped.)

11

un poco più

mf

Pi - e Je - su Do - mi - ne, do - na_ e - is re - qui - em, do - na_ e - is

mf

dim.

(Man.)

16

p

p *dolce*

re - qui - em, do - na,_ do - na, Do - mi - ne,

p

pp

(Ped.)

(Man.)

21 *poco cresc.* *p*

do-na e-is re - qui-em sem-pi-ter-nam re - qui-em sem - pi-ter - nam

pp

26 *mf*

re - qui-em, sem - pi-ter - nam re - qui-em. Pi - e, pi - e

mf

(Ped.) (Man.)

30

Je - su, pi - e Je-su Do - mi-ne, do - na e - is, do - na e - is

35 *poco rit.*

sem - pi-ter - nam re - qui-em, sem-pi - ter - nam re - qui - em.

pp *poco rit.*

(Ped.) (ca. 3')

50. *Gebet*

Herr, schicke was du willt

Prayer (*Lord, Send What Thou Deem'st Best*)

Hugo Wolf (1860–1903)
Text: Eduard Mörike
Org.-Arr.: Max Reger

Getragen
(Sostenuto)
Org.*)
II. Man.
p
mf
Ped.

6
(fromm und innig /
with devotion and fervour)
Herr!_ Schi-cke was du willt, ein
Lord, send what Thou deem'st best be
f
ff
p
III. Man.
pp

11
Lie-bes o-der Lei - des; ich bin ver-gnügt, dass bei - - des aus dei - nen
it or joy or griev - ing; I wait Thy will, be-liev - - ing that both Thy
f

*) Klavierbegleitung: Anhang S. 160 / *Piano accompaniment: see Appendix, p. 160*

16
Hän - den quillt. Wol - lest mit Freu - den und wol - lest mit Lei - den mich
love at - test. Not with - out mea - sure give sad - ness or plea - sure, all -
pp
mf
sf
21
nicht ü - ber - schüt - ten! Doch in der Mit - ten,
- mer - ci - ful Fa - ther! For mid - way ra - ther,
II. Man. (4')
(zart und ausdrucksvoll /
delicately and with expression)
p
pp
III. Man. (8')
25
doch in der Mit - ten liegt hol - des Be - schei - den.
for mid - way ra - ther, lies heart's ease pure trea - sure.
dim.
29
ppp
III. Man. (8')
(ca. 3')

Anhang I
Klavierfassungen zu den Orgelbearbeitungen

Appendix I
Piano versions of the organ arrangements

5a. *He Shall Feed His Flock*

Er weidet seine Herde

Georg Friedrich Händel (1685–1759)
Messiah, HWV 56
Piano-Arr.: Julius Stern

Piano

4

He shall feed His flock like a shep - - herd, and
Er wei - det sei - ne Her - de, ein gu - ter Hir - te, und

7

He shall ga - ther the lambs with His arm, with His arm,
sam - melt sei - ne Läm - mer in sei - nen Arm, in sei - nen Arm.

f

10

and car - ry them in His bos - om, and
Er nimmt sie mit Er - bar - men in sei - nen Schoß, und

p

13
gen - tly lead those that are with young; and gen - tly lead, and
lei - tet sanft, die ge - bä - ren soll, und lei - tet sanft, und
16
gen - tly lead those that are with young.
lei - tet sanft, die ge - bä - ren soll.
f
19
Come un - to Him all ye that la - bour, come
Kommt her zu ihm, die ihr müh - se - lig seid, kommt
p
22
un - to Him that are hea - vy la - den, and He will give you rest.
her zu ihm, mit Trau - rig - keit Be - lad - ne, denn er ver - leiht euch Ruh.

25
Take His yoke up - on you, and learn of Him, for
Nehmt auf euch sein Joch und ler - net von ihm, denn
p
28
He is meek and low - ly of heart, and ye shall find rest, and
er ist sanft und de - muts - voll, dann fin - det ihr Ruh, für
31
ye shall find rest un - to your souls.
eu - er Herz, für eu - er Herz.
f
34
(ca. 5')

9a. *Die Ehre Gottes aus der Natur*

All Nature Sings God's Praises

Ludwig van Beethoven (1770–1827)
Op. 48 Nr. 4
Text: Chr. F. Gellert
Ed.: Roland Erben

Majestätisch und erhaben

Piano

ff

Die Him - mel rüh - men des
The bound - less Hea - vens ex -

5

E - wi - gen Eh - re, ihr Schall pflanzt sei - nen Na - men fort. Ihn
- tol the Al - migh - ty, their thun - der ech - oes forth His name. The

sf p f sf p

11

rühmt der Erd - kreis, ihn prei - sen die Mee - re; ver - nimm, o
earth ex - alts Him, the seas sing His prais - es, take heed, O

f sf

16

Mensch, ihr gött - lich Wort! Wer
man; their mess - age hear! What

sf sf sf sf pp (sim.)

21
trägt der Him-mel un-zähl-ba-re Ster-ne? Wer führt die
power rules o-ver thy con-stel-la-tions? Who guides the
cresc.
26
Sonn' aus ih-rem Zelt? Sie kömmt und leuch-tet und
sun up there on high? Its rays smile down on the
pp
cresc.
f
31
lacht uns von fer-ne und läuft den Weg gleich als ein Held, und
world, on all na-tions, tri-um-phant-ly it rides the sky, tri-
sf
p
f
37
läuft den Weg gleich als ein Held.
-um-phant-ly it rides the sky.
ff
sf
sf
sf
ff
(ca. 3')

27a. *Ave Maria*

Ellens Gesang III / Hymne an die Jungfrau

Hymn to the Maiden

Franz Schubert (1797–1828)
D 839
Text: Walter Scott
Ed.: Roland Erben

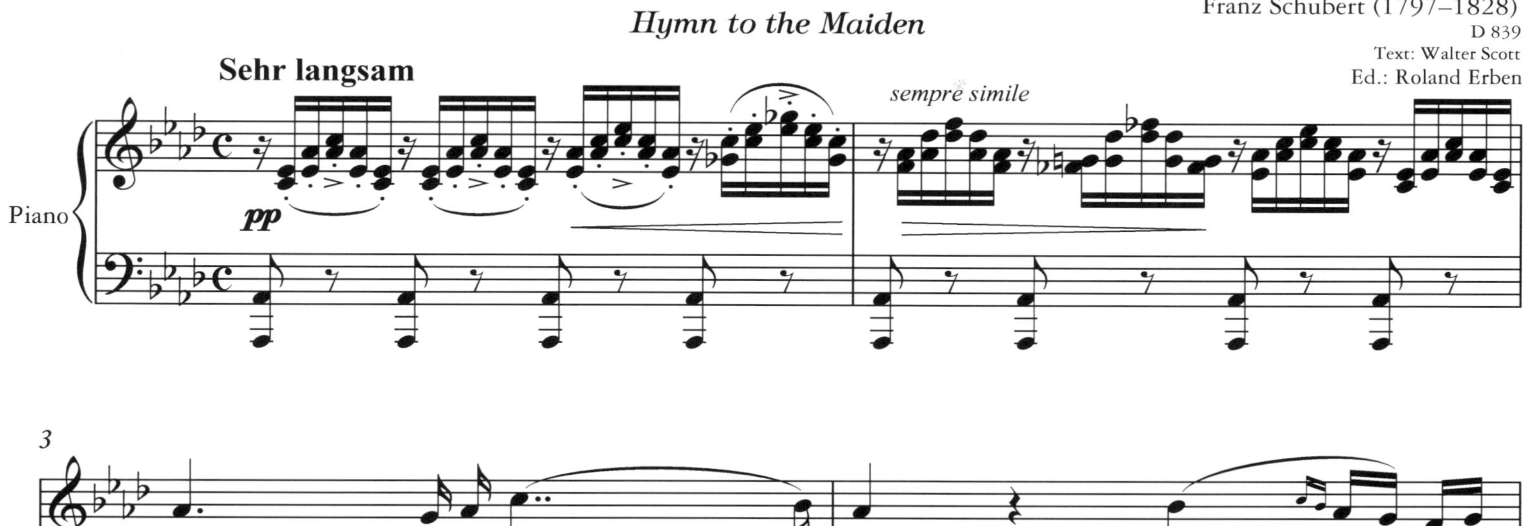
Sehr langsam
sempre simile
Piano
pp

3
1. A - - ve Ma-ri - - - - a! Jung - - frau
1. A - - ve Ma-ri - - - - a, Mai - - den

5
mild, er-hö - re_ei-ner Jung-frau Fle - hen, aus die - sem Fel-sen starr und
mild. Ah! lis - ten_to a mai-den's pray - er, For Thou canst hear a-mid_the
3
3

7
wild soll_mein Ge-bet_zu dir_hin-we - - - - hen. Wir
wild, 'Tis Thou, 'tis Thou canst save a - mid des-pair. We

schla - fen si - cher bis zum Mor - gen, ob Men - schen noch so grau - sam sind. O
slum - ber safe - ly till the mor - row, Though ba - nished, out - cast and_ re - viled: Oh
Jung - frau, sieh der Jung - frau Sor - gen, o Mut - ter, hör ein bit - tend Kind!
Maid - en, see a maid - en's sor - row, Oh Moth - er, hear_ a supp - liant child!
fp
pp
A - - ve Ma - ri - - - a!
2. A - - ve Ma - ri - -
2. A - - ve Ma - ri - -
-a! Rei - - ne_ Magd! Der Er - de_und der Luft Dä -
-a, Stain - - less_ styl'd! Each fiend of_ air or earth - ly

19 -mo - nen, von dei - nes Au - ges Huld ver - jagt, sie_ kön - nen hier nicht bei uns
es - sence, from this their won - ted haunt ex - il'd, Shall flee be - fore_ Thy ho - ly

21 woh - - - - nen. Wir woll'n uns still dem Schick - sal beu - gen, da
pres - - - - ence. We bow be - neath our cares o'er la - den, To

23 uns dein heil' - ger Trost an - weht; der Jung - frau wol - le hold dich nei - gen, dem
thy dear guid - ance rec - on - cil'd, Then hear, Oh Maid, a sim - ple mai - den, And

25 Kind, das für_ den Va - ter fleht! A - - ve Ma - ri - -
for a fa - ther hear a child! A - - ve Ma - ri - -

27 -a!
-a!

43a. *Im Abendrot*

Evening Glow

Franz Schubert (1797–1828)
D 799
Text: Karl Lappe
Ed.: Roland Erben

Langsam, feierlich

Piano

pp

con Pedale

Oh, wie schön ist

6

dei - ne Welt, Va - ter, wenn sie gol-den strah - let, wenn dein Glanz her-

11

- nie - der - fällt, und den Staub mit Schim-mer ma - let,

15

wenn das Rot, das in der Wol - ke_ blinkt, in mein stil - les_ Fens - ter sinkt.

ppp

19
Könnt ich kla - gen, könnt ich za - gen? ir - re sein an dir und
mf
24
mir? Nein, ich will im Bu - sen tra - gen dei - nen
f
28
Him - mel schon all - hier, und dies Herz, eh es zu - sam - men bricht, trinkt noch Glut und
p
pp
32
schlürft noch Licht, trinkt noch Glut und schlürft noch Licht.
ppp
dimin.
(ca. 3')

50a. *Gebet*

Herr, schicke was du willt

Prayer (*Lord, Send What Thou Deem'st Best*)

Hugo Wolf (1860–1903)
Text: Eduard Mörike
Ed.: Roland Erben

Getragen
(Sostenuto)
Piano
p

5
mf
f
ff
p

9
(fromm und innig /
with devotion and fervour)
Herr! schi - cke was du willt, ein Lie - bes o - der Lei - des;
Lord, send what Thou deem'st best, be it or joy or griev - ing;
pp

13
ich bin ver - gnügt, dass bei - - des aus dei - nen Hän - den quillt.
I wait Thy will, be - liev - - ing that both Thy love at - test.
f
pp

17
Wol - lest mit Freu - den und wol - lest mit Lei - den mich
Not with - out mea - sure give sad - ness or plea - sure, all -
mf
sf
21
nicht ü - ber - schüt - ten! Doch in der Mit - ten,
- mer - ci - ful Fa - ther! For mid - way ra - ther,
p
pp
25
doch in der Mit - ten liegt hol - des Be - schei - den.
for mid - way ra - ther, lies heart's ease pure trea - sure.
dim.
29
ppp
(ca. 3')

Anmerkungen zu den einzelnen Stücken

1.

Heinrich Schütz, *Bringt her dem Herren* (SWV 283) ist die Nr. 1 der *Kleinen geistlichen Konzerte*, die für Singstimme und Continuo komponiert ist. Aufgrund seines lebendigen Duktus' eignet sich das Stück für verschiedene Anlässe, vorwiegend im kirchlichen Rahmen, besonders auch für den Beginn einer Feier. Die Continuoaussetzung stammt vom Herausgeber. Originaltonart C-Dur.

QUELLE: Alte Schütz-Gesamtausgabe (1887) und Ausgabe von Wilhelm Ehmann und Hans Hoffmann, Kassel 1963. – Englische Textfassung von Jean Lunn (Schütz, *Five Short Sacred Concertos for Voice and Organ*, Edition Peters No. 6894, New York, 1966).

2.

J. S. Bach, *Wachet auf, ruft uns die Stimme*, ein Satz aus der gleichnamigen Kantate Nr. 140, original für Tenor, Streicher (Violinen und Violen unisono in der Oberstimme) und Basso continuo. Bach verbindet hier die Choralmelodie mit einer melodisch ausdrucksvollen Begleitung, deren Motivik in den Anfangstakten von starker Prägnanz ist. Bachs eigene Bearbeitung dieses Stückes für Orgel allein (BWV 645) wurde zum Vergleich mit herangezogen. Die kleinen Noten der vorliegenden Ausgabe sind Fülltöne, die bei der Ausführung mit Orgel wegbleiben sollten. Originaltonart Es-Dur.

QUELLE: Klavierauszug, Edition Breitkopf; Neue Bach-Ausgabe *NBA* I/27. – Englische Textfassung von Charles Sanford Terry (1864–1936).

3.

J. S. Bach, *Bekennen will ich seinen Namen* (BWV 200) ist als einzelner Satz überliefert und wohl als Teil einer nicht weiter erhaltenen Kirchenkantate anzusehen. Diese schöne Alt-Arie, die ebensogut von Mezzosopran, ggf. auch von einer hell timbrierten Baritonstimme gesungen werden kann, stammt aus Bachs letzten Schaffensjahren und wurde erst rund 200 Jahre nach ihrem Entstehen aufgefunden und veröffentlicht. Der Klaviersatz ist nach Bachs Partitur, in der zwei Violinen und B. c. vorgesehen sind, vom Herausgeber der vorliegenden Sammlung erstellt. Die beiden Violinen und die Basslinie erscheinen im Normalstich, harmonische Auffüllungen im Kleinstich.

QUELLE: J. S. Bach, *Bekennen will ich seinen Namen*, Partitur und Stimmen, hrsg. von Ludwig Landshoff, Leipzig 1935, Edition Peters Nr. 4209.

4.

J. S. Bach, *Schafe können sicher weiden*: aus der *„Jagdkantate"*, BWV 208. Wie bei Nr. 2 (*Wachet auf*) hat Bach auch hier die Solostimme mit einer charakteristischen Begleitung unterlegt, deren Hauptmotiv stärker im Ohr bleibt als die Melodie des Gesangsparts. In den Takten 30–40 ist eine Umtextierung vorgenommen worden; der Originaltext der weltlichen Kantate lautet an dieser Stelle: *„Wo Regenten wohl regieren, kann man Ruh' und Frieden spüren, und was Länder glücklich macht."* Originale Instrumentation: Sopran, 2 Blockflöten und Continuo. Unsere Bearbeitung gibt den Part der beiden Blockflöten im Normalstich wieder, wobei zur spieltechnischen Erleichterung die kleiner gesetzten Noten weggelassen werden können. Passagen, die im Original nur mit Continuo begleitet sind, erscheinen in der RH durchgehend im Kleinstich. Originaltonart B-Dur.

QUELLE: Neue Bach-Ausgabe *NBA* I/35. – Englische Textfassung vom Herausgeber nach Charles Sanford Terry (1864–1936).

5.

G. F. Händel, *Er weidet seine Herde*: Die berühmte Sopranarie aus dem *Messias* eignet sich zur Darbietung bei verschiedenen Festlichkeiten, wo sie einen stimmungsvollen Höhepunkt bilden kann. Wegen des ruhigen Tempos ist als Begleitinstrument die Orgel vorzuziehen. Von Händel selbst existiert eine Variante dieser Arie, die in F-Dur beginnt (Altstimme) und bei *„Kommt her zu ihm"* zur Originaltonart B-Dur zurückkehrt (Sopran). In vorliegender Bearbeitung wird hingegen die Altlage durchweg beibehalten. Da die originale Spieldauer von ca. 8 Minuten sich in vielen Fällen als zu lang erweist, wurde das Stück hier um jene Teile gekürzt, die Händel als ausgeschriebene Wiederholungen notiert hat (insgesamt 20 Takte). Orgelsatz vom Herausgeber. Klavierfassung im Anhang, Seite 150.

QUELLE: G. F. Händel, *Messiah*, HWV 56, Ausgabe von Donald Burrows, Edition Peters No. 7317. Deutsche Textversion von Julius Stern (Edition Peters Nr. 60).

6.

G. F. Händel, *Where e'er You Walk* ist dem II. Akt des Oratoriums *Semele*, HWV 58, entnommen, aufgrund ihres Textes bietet sich die Arie gut zur Gestaltung von Hochzeitsfeiern an. Der Orgelsatz wurde nach Händels Streichersatz erstellt. Originaltonart B-Dur.

QUELLE: G. F. Händel, *Semele*, Ausgabe von Fr. Chrysander, Bd. 7, 1860.

7.

G. F. Händel, *Verdi prati, selve amene* ist eine Mezzosopran-Arie aus Händels italienischer Oper *Alcina* (HWV 34), die 1735 entstand. Die entsprechende Rolle (Ruggiero) wurde damals von einer Männerstimme (Kastrat) gesungen. Die Arie handelt von der vergehenden Schönheit der Natur und zeugt von Händels Fähigkeit, mit einfachen musikalischen Mitteln eine intensive Aussage zu schaffen. In ihrer ausdrucksvollen Schlichtheit eignet sie sich zum Vortrag bei Festlichkeiten verschiedener Art. Der Begleitsatz folgt Händels Partiturnotation (Violinen I/II, Viola, Continuo). Die Kleinstichnoten sind Fülltöne zur Abrundung des Klavierklangs. Kleine Noten in Klammern können bei Orgelwiedergabe im Pedal mitgespielt werden. Englischer Text von Nathan Haskiel Dole (1852–1935).

QUELLE: G. F. Händel, *Alcina*, Ausgabe von F. Chrysander, Bd. 86, 1868. – Englische Textversion aus: Ausgabe für Stimme und Klavier von Ebenezer Prout, Oliver Ditson Company, 1905.

8.  

Giuseppe Giordani, *Caro mio ben*: Dieses Liebeslied erreichte bereits im 18. Jahrhundert große Popularität, u. a. durch die Darbietungen des italienischen Kastraten Gasparo Pacchierotti (1778 in London). Bisweilen wird die Komposition auch Giordanis Bruder Tommaso (ca. 1730–1806) zugeschrieben. Die Auszierungsvorschläge in den Takten 19, 22, 29 und 30 (Kleinstichnoten) stammen vom Herausgeber. Originaltonart F-Dur.

Quelle: *A Selection of Italian Arias 1600–1800*, Vol. I, hrsg. von Anthony Lewis, Hohe Stimme, ABRSM 1983.

9.

L. v. Beethoven, *Die Ehre Gottes aus der Natur* („*Die Himmel rühmen*") ist die Nr. 4 aus den *Sechs Liedern nach Texten von Gellert* Op. 48. Das Lied, von dem auch mehrere Chorbearbeitungen existieren, symbolisiert die Größe der göttlichen Schöpfung und kann bei vielen Anlässen gesungen werden. Es ist vor allem ein Repertoirestück vieler Tenor-Solisten. Orgelbearbeitung vom Herausgeber. Originaltonart C-Dur. Klaviersatz im Anhang, Seite 153.

Quelle: L. v. Beethoven, *Ausgewählte Lieder*, Edition Peters Nr. 180 (dort mit weiteren Strophen) sowie Neue Beethoven Gesamtausgabe XII/1. – Englische Textfassung von Frederick Fuller, aus: *The Art of Song*. Grades 1–5. Edition Peters No. 7441, London 1994.

10.

L. van Beethoven, *Ich liebe dich, so wie du mich* („*Zärtliche Liebe*"), WoO 123. Ein fast schlichtes, aber zeitlos schönes Liebeslied des 27-jährigen Beethoven, das bei Hochzeiten genauso wie bei Silbernen/Goldenen Hochzeiten gerne als Ständchen dargeboten wird. Der Text stammt von Karl Friedrich Wilhelm Herrosee (1754–1823), der als Prediger und Superintendent tätig war und auch als Verfasser geistlicher Texte hervortrat. Beethoven hat im Autograph keinerlei Dynamik eingetragen; die in vorliegende Ausgabe übernommenen, aus späteren Drucken stammenden Angaben sind daher nur als Vorschläge zu betrachten.

Als Begleitsatz ist die originale Klavierfassung abgedruckt, bei einer Wiedergabe auf der Orgel sollte bei oktavierten Passagen die Unteroktave weggelassen und die beiden Schlussakkorde ausgedünnt werden. Originaltonart G-Dur.

Quelle: L. v. Beethoven, *Ausgewählte Lieder*, Edition Peters Nr. 180 (dort mit weiteren Strophen) sowie Neue Beethoven Gesamtausgabe XII/1. – Englische Textfassung aus einer Einzelausgabe des Verlages J. André, Offenbach (ca. 1870).

11.

Felix Mendelssohn Bartholdy, *O for the Wings of a Dove / O könnt' ich fliegen wie Tauben dahin*, WoO 15 (Werknummer nach der Neuen Leipziger Ausgabe: B 49). Die Komposition *Hear My Prayer / Hör' mein Bitten* für Sopran solo, gemischten Chor und Orgel ist auf Texte aus dem Buch der Psalmen (Altes Testament, Psalm 55) komponiert, die der Engländer William Bartholomew (1793–1867) für Mendelssohn zusammengestellt hatte. Die Komposition ist vor allem im angelsächsischen Raum sehr beliebt.

Bei der vorliegenden Fassung handelt es sich um eine gekürzte Version, bestehend aus dem Anfang von *Hear My Prayer* und dem gesamten lyrischen Abschnitt *O for the Wings of a Dove*, woraus vom chorischen Teil die Oberstimme übernommen wurde. Der Orgelsatz folgt Mendelssohns originalem Orgelbegleitsatz. Die Textstelle „*In die Wüste eilt ich dann fort*" wurde zwecks allgemeiner Verwendbarkeit geändert in „*Auf den Flügeln eilt ich dann fort*". Originaltonart G-Dur.

Quelle: Ausgabe Breitkopf & Härtel, Leipzig 1875. – Englische Textfassung aus: Mendelssohn, *Hear my Prayer. The Choralist*, No. 300, Boosey & Co. (ca. 1896).

12. 

Robert Schumann, *Widmung* („*Du meine Seele*"): Dieses Stück, das den Liederzyklus *Myrthen* Op. 25 einleitet, überreichte Schumann seiner Braut Clara als Geschenk zum Hochzeitstag (12. September 1840). Es ist seither eines der bekanntesten Liebeslieder der Romantik geblieben. Der Text stammt von Friedrich Rückert. Einrichtung des Klavierparts für Orgel vom Herausgeber. Originaltonart As-Dur.

Quelle: R. Schumann, *Lieder*, Bd. I, hrsg. von Max Friedländer, Edition Peters Nr. 2383b. – Englische Textfassung vom Herausgeber unter Mitarbeit von Denette Whitter.

13.

Robert Schumann, *Du Ring an meinem Finger*: Im Zyklus *Frauenliebe und Leben* Op. 42 kommt diesem Lied als Sinnbild des Lebensbundes eine besondere Stellung zu. Der Klaviersatz konnte mit wenigen Abänderungen für die Orgel übernommen werden (so wurden etwa in der LH, T. 25–30, die Tonwiederholungen durch ausgehaltene Töne ersetzt). Text: Adelbert von Chamisso.

Quelle: R. Schumann, *Frauenliebe und Leben*, Urtext, hrsg. von H. J. Köhler, Edition Peters Nr. 9536. – Englische Textfassung von Lewis Novra und Louis Charles Elson, aus: *Schumann Album, 40 ausgewählte Lieder*, Henry Litolff's Verlag, Braunschweig 1887 (Collection Litolff Nr. 1691).

14.

Louis Roessel, *Kavatine* („*Wenn ich mit Menschen- und mit Engelzungen*"): Roessel ist als Komponist heute vergessen, sein Opus 25 (Untertitel: *Trauungsgesang*) wird jedoch im deutschsprachigen Raum nach wie vor oft aufgeführt bei Feierlichkeiten, nicht zuletzt wegen der starken Aussagekraft des Textes. Er stammt aus dem Neuen Testament, 1. Korintherbrief des Paulus, Kap. 13, Vs. 1–3, 12–13. Als Vorlage für die Orgeleinrichtung diente der originale Klavierpart. Originaltonart G-Dur.

Quelle: *Hosianna, Ausgewählte geistliche Lieder und Arien*, Lienau Verlag, Nr. 124.

15.

Eugen Hildach, *Wo du hingehst*: Dem Lied liegt ein Textausschnitt aus dem alten Testament (Buch Ruth) zugrunde, der vielfach vertont wurde (siehe auch Lieder Nr. 18 und 19) und bei Hochzeiten wie auch Hochzeitsjubiläen sehr beliebt ist. Hildach war Gesangslehrer am Konservatorium in Breslau und selbst Konzertsänger. Mit seiner Ehefrau Anna, einer Mezzosopranistin, veranstaltete er Liederabende und Oratoriumsaufführungen. Von seinen Liedern ist das vorliegende Op. 8 bis heute das bekannteste geblieben. Die

Erstausgabe ist mit Klavier- und gesonderter Orgelbegleitung versehen, aus ihr wurde der Orgelsatz sowie die englische Textversion von John Bernhoff übernommen. Text: Altes Testament, Buch Ruth, Kap. 1, Vs. 16–17. Originaltonart D-Dur.

QUELLE: Erstdruck, Heinrichshofen's Verlag, Magdeburg 1898.

16. 

Edvard Grieg, *Ich liebe dich*. Dieses berühmte Liebeslied ist die Nr. 3 aus den *Melodien des Herzens* Op. 5 nach Texten von Hans Christian Andersen. Neben dem dänischen Text enthielt bereits die Erstausgabe eine deutsche Übertragung von Franz von Holstein, die bis heute sehr verbreitet ist. Im Klavierbegleitsatz, der sich für eine Orgelwiedergabe kaum eignet, sind einige Töne, die sich schwer greifen lassen, eingeklammert, sie können zur Erleichterung gegebenenfalls weggelassen werden.

QUELLE: *Edvard Grieg Gesamtausgabe*, Bd. 14, daraus auch die englische Textfassung von W. H. Halverson (leicht modifiziert).

17. 

Guy d' Hardelot, *Because*: Ein in den angelsächsischen Ländern und den USA sehr verbreiteter Song, der im Stil einer *show tune* für Gesang und Klavier komponiert ist. Guy d' Hardelot (bürgerlicher Name: Helen Rhodes), Tochter einer französischen Mutter und eines englischen Vaters, studierte mit 15 Jahren bereits am Pariser Conservatoire, später wirkte sie in London als Gesangslehrerin und war auch als Komponistin von Liedern erfolgreich. Der ursprüngliche französische Text von *Because* stammt von der Autorin selbst, doch wurde das Lied vor allem in der englischen Übertragung von Edward Teschemacher international bekannt. – Die klein gestochenen Noten in der Gesangsstimme sind Alternativvorschläge des Herausgebers. Als Begleitinstrument eignet sich hier nur das Klavier. Der Erstdruck enthält zahlreiche Pedalangaben, diese wurden nicht übernommen. Originaltonart C-Dur.

QUELLE: Ausgabe Chappell & Co., 1900, Nr. 21782.

18.

Paul Dessau, *Entreat Me Not*: Dessau schrieb dieses Lied 1945 in Hollywood zur Hochzeit seiner Tochter Eva. Den Text, in englischer Fassung, entnahm er dem Buch Ruth des Alten Testaments (Kap. 1, Vs. 16–17).

QUELLE: P. Dessau, *Lieder aus dem Nachlass*, Urtext, hrsg. von Axel Bauni, Edition Peters Nr. 11098, Frankfurt/M. 2009.

19.

Flor Peeters, *Wedding Song*: Über dieses sowohl als Sololied als auch in einer chorischen Variante (jeweils mit Klavier- oder Orgelbegleitung) existierende Stück schreibt der Herausgeber der Erstausgabe (1962): „Flor Peeters' Wedding Song ist eine bemerkenswerte Komposition, die unser verhältnismäßig schmales Repertoire herausragender Solo- und Chormusik für kirchliche Hochzeiten erweitert und bereichert." Text: Buch Ruth des Alten Testaments (Kap. 1, Vs. 16–17). Einrichtung des englischen Textes von Hugh Ross.

QUELLE: Fl. Peeters, *Wedding Song, edited by Walter E. Buszin*, C. F. Peters Corporation No. 6244c, New York 1962.

20. 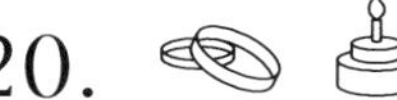

Alan Hovhaness, *Love's Philosophy*: Hovhaness, amerikanischer Komponist armenischer Herkunft, zählt in Amerika zu den meistgespielten Tonschöpfern. Stilistisch greift er sowohl auf armenische Volksmusik als auch auf europäische Traditionen, insbesondere der Renaissancezeit, zurück. Auch andere Einflüsse, etwa aus der Postromantik oder der indischen Musik, haben in seinem Werk Niederschlag gefunden. Hovhaness schrieb *Love's Philosophy*, sein Op. 370, im Jahr 1984 zur Hochzeit eines mit ihm befreundeten Ehepaares. Der Text stammt von dem britischen Dichter Percy Bysshe Shelley (1792–1822). Die Originaltonart ist a-Moll, eine Quarte höher.

QUELLE: Ausgabe Edition Peters No. 67522, C. F. Peters Corporation, New York 1994.

21.

Stefan Nilsson, *Fly With Me (Lenas sång)*: Als Beitrag aus unserem Jahrhundert konnte ein Lied aus dem schwedischen Film *Wie im Himmel* in die vorliegende Sammlung mit einbezogen werden. Es ist seit seinem Erscheinen (2004) nicht nur von Sängerinnen populärer Musik in ihr Repertoire genommen worden. Stefan Nilsson wurde vor allem durch seine Filmmusiken bekannt; er komponierte jedoch auch in anderen Genres wie Ballett und Oper.

QUELLE: Einzelausgabe für Solostimme und Klavier, Gehrmans Musikförlag, Nr. 10814. Abdruck mit freundlicher Genehmigung.

22. 

J. S. Bach, *Jesus bleibet meine Freude* (aus Kantate Nr. 147): Dieser berühmte Choralsatz mit seiner charakteristischen, fließenden Triolenbegleitung ist in zahlreichen, oft auch rein instrumentalen Bearbeitungen verbreitet. Er gehört zu den Stücken, die „universell", d. h. für freudige wie auch für Traueranlässe geeignet sind. Bach hat ihn instrumentiert für vierstimmigen gemischten Chor, Streicher, Oboe (Violine I verdoppelnd), Trompete (die Sopranstimme verdoppelnd) und Continuo. Unsere Einrichtung für Singstimme und Orgel übernimmt den Sopranpart als Sologesangsstimme und – soweit möglich und spielbar – den originalen Streichersatz. Die klein gesetzten Noten sind für die Wiedergabe auf dem Klavier gedacht, können zur Erleichterung aber auch weggelassen werden. Originaltonart G-Dur.

QUELLE: Neue Bach-Ausgabe *NBA* I/28. – Englische Textfassung von Charles Sanford Terry (1864–1936).

23.

Bach-Gounod, *Ave Maria*: Zu J. S. Bachs Eingangspräludium zum *Wohltemperierten Klavier*, Teil I, schrieb der französische Opernkomponist Charles Gounod im Jahr 1852 eine *„Mélodie religieuse" (adaptée au 1er Prélude de J. S. Bach)*, die weltweit populär wurde und beinahe zu jedem möglichen Anlass aufgeführt werden kann. Der Erstdruck enthält die Widmung an eine französische Opernsängerin (Mme Miolan-Carvalho), doch kann das Stück von einer Tenorstimme ebenfalls gesungen werden. In dem original in G-Dur stehenden Satz hat Gounod die Takte 20–38 in sehr tiefe Lage gesetzt, daher wurde die RH hier aus klanglichen Gründen eine Oktave höher gelegt. Der kursive Alternativtext ab Takt 24 eignet sich speziell für die evangelische Kirchenmusikpraxis.

Quelle: J. S. Bach / Ch. Gounod, *Ave Maria*. Ausgabe in drei Tonarten (neben G-Dur auch F-Dur und D-Dur), Urtext, hrsg. von Roger Nichols, Edition Peters Nr. 7668.

24.

Antonio Vivaldi, *Domine Deus*: Auch dieser Satz (aus dem zehnsätzigen *Gloria*, RV 589) hat sich bei unterschiedlichen Anlässen bewährt. Vivaldi hat ihn für Sopran, Oboe (oder Violine) solo und Continuo instrumentiert. Im vorliegenden Begleitsatz für Orgel allein sind die klein gestochenen Noten harmonische Ausfüllungen in der Art eines ausgesetzten Continuoparts. Originaltonart C-Dur.

Quelle: A. Vivaldi, *Gloria*. Partitur und Klavierauszug, Urtext, hrsg. von Klaus Burmeister, Edition Peters Nr. 8866 und 8867.

25.

G. F. Händel, *„Largo“* (*Ombra mai fù*) aus der Oper *Xerxes* (orig.: *Serse*, HWV 40): In dieser kurzen, die Oper einleitenden Arie, die zu Händels populärsten Stücken zählt, wird ein angenehmer, Schatten spendender Platz unter einer Platane besungen. Es hat nicht an Versuchen gefehlt, den schlichten Text, auch in anderen Sprachen, durch neue Worte zu ersetzen, doch konnte sich keine Alternative durchsetzen. Bei Bedarf kann der italienische Originaltext durch den aus späterer Zeit stammenden, hier als 2. Strophe wiedergegebenen Text (*„Tu sei il mio ciel“*) ersetzt werden. Um einer festlichen Darbietung mehr Raum zu geben, können auch beide Strophen gesungen werden. Der Orgelsatz folgt weitgehend dem originalen Streichersatz. Bei einmanualiger Ausführung (und Wiedergabe auf dem Klavier) übernimmt die LH die Bassstimme und einige tiefer liegende Töne des darüberliegenden Systems, die RH spielt zusammenfassend die beiden oberen Systeme. Originaltonart F-Dur.

Quelle: G. F. Händel, *Serse*. Chrysander-Ausgabe, Bd. 92, Leipzig 1884.

26.

L. van Beethoven, *Bitten* (*„Gott, deine Güte reicht so weit“*): Beethoven schrieb die *Sechs Lieder* Op. 48 auf Texte von Christian Fürchtegott Gellert (1715–1769) im Jahr 1803 und widmete sie dem Grafen Johann Georg von Browne anlässlich des Todes von dessen Frau Anna Margarete. – Der originale Klaviersatz trägt bereits orgelmäßige Züge und konnte daher für die Wiedergabe auf der Orgel weitgehend beibehalten werden. Originaltonart E-Dur.

Quelle: L. v. Beethoven, *Ausgewählte Lieder*, Edition Peters Nr. 180 (dort mit weiteren Strophen) sowie Neue Beethoven-Gesamtausgabe XII/1. – Englische Textfassung nach einer historischen Ausgabe (19. Jhdt.).

27.

Franz Schubert, *Ave Maria*, D 839: Im Jahr 1825 vertonte Schubert mehrere Ausschnitte aus dem Versepos *The Lady of the Lake* („Das Fräulein vom See“) des schottischen Dichters Sir Walter Scott (1771–1832) in deutscher Übertragung von D. Adam Storck. Das Lied ist original betitelt als *Ellen's Gesang III / Hymne an die Jungfrau*. In Scotts Gedicht ist Ellen, die Tochter des Grafen Douglas, aus Furcht vor dem ungeliebten Freier Roderick in die Wildnis geflohen. Dieser hört eines Abends ihren Gesang, von einer Harfe begleitet, über den See klingen und ist sich nicht sicher, „ob Ellen oder ein Engel singt“. – Für die Wiedergabe auf der Orgel wurde der Klaviersatz in einen triomäßigen, leicht ausführbaren Satz umgestaltet. Die Kleinstichnoten sind nur auf zweimanualigen Orgeln realisierbar. Originaler Klaviersatz im Anhang, S. 155.

Quelle: F. Schubert, *Lieder*, Neue Ausgabe von Dietrich Fischer-Dieskau und Elmar Budde, Bd. III, Ausgabe für mittlere Stimme, Edition Peters Nr. 8305b (dort 3 Strophen).

28.

Ferdinand Hiller, *Gebet* (*„Herr, den ich tief im Herzen trage“*) Op. 46 Nr. 1: Hiller, der mit Mendelssohn und Schumann befreundet war, verlieh dem rheinischen Musikleben seiner Zeit wichtige Impulse. Als Komponist ist er hauptsächlich durch das *Gebet* lebendig geblieben, wozu auch der bekenntnishafte, Zuversicht ausdrückende Text von Emanuel Geibel (1815–1884) einen wesentlichen Teil beigetragen hat. Das Lied eignet sich besonders für Firmung/Konfirmation und andere kirchliche Anlässe. Der Begleitsatz ist bereits im Original vom Komponisten sowohl für Klavier als auch für Orgel ausgewiesen. Originaltonart F-Dur.

Quelle: *Hosianna, Ausgewählte geistliche Lieder und Arien*, Lienau-Verlag. – Englische Textfassung von Alma Strettell (19. Jhdt.).

29.

César Franck, *Panis angelicus*: Franck schuf diese berühmte Komposition im Jahr 1872 und fügte sie nachträglich in seine schon 12 Jahre zuvor entstandene *Messe à trois voix* Op. 12 ein. *Panis angelicus* („Das Engelsbrot“) ist original instrumentiert für Solostimme, Orgel, Harfe und Violoncello. Im vorliegenden Begleitsatz für Orgel allein wurden die Violoncellostimme eine Oktave höher gelegt und der Harfenpart durch Staccatotöne angedeutet. – Als Textvorlage diente dem Komponisten die 6. Strophe aus Thomas von Aquins Fronleichnams-Hymnus *Sacris Solemnis* (13. Jahrhundert). Auf Deutsch lautet der Text etwa: „Das Engelsbrot wird Brot der Menschen. Das Himmelsbrot setzt den irdischen Gestalten ein Ende. O wunderbares Geschehen! Es nimmt der arme und bescheidene Diener den Herren in sich auf.“ Originaltonart A-Dur.

Quelle: C. Franck, *Messe à trois voix*. Partitur-Erstdruck, Verlag E. Repos / Bornemann, Paris 1872.

30.

Anton Bruckner, *Ave Maria*: Mit seinen typischen Modulationen spiegelt die 1882 entstandene Vertonung den reifen Kompositionsstil des Meisters wider. Bruckner widmete das Stück *Fräulein Luise Hochleitner*, der Schwägerin seines Schülers Camillo Horn. Der Begleitsatz entspricht Bruckners Original (für „Klavier, Orgel oder Harmonium“), die Halsierung und Verteilung der Manualstimmen erfolgen allerdings gemäß einer Ausführung mit Pedal. Die klein gestochenen Noten in der Singstimme (T. 72–74) sind ein Alternativvorschlag des Herausgebers.

Quelle: A. Bruckner, *Kleine Kirchenmusikwerke 1835–1892*, Musikwissenschaftlicher Verlag der Internationalen Bruckner-Gesellschaft, Wien 1984 (= Kritische Gesamtausgabe, Bd. 21).

31.

Camille Saint-Saëns, *Deus Abraham*: Das 1885 komponierte Stück ist für Sopran, gemischten Chor, Orgel und eine Harfenstimme ad libitum gesetzt, die Einrichtung für Singstimme und Orgel stammt vom Herausgeber. In den Takten 21–32 wurde vom Chorsatz die Oberstimme in vorliegende Fassung übernommen. Originaltonart F-Dur.

QUELLE: Erstdruck, Durand, Paris 1892.

32.

Antonín Dvořák, *Gott ist mein Hirte*: Dieses Lied ist die Nr. 4 aus den *Biblischen Liedern* Op. 99, komponiert 1894 auf Worte aus Psalm 23. Die Vertonung ist in Art eines Anrufs bzw. einer Monodie mit sparsamer Begleitung angelegt, die der Solostimme viel Gestaltungsspielraum lässt. Der Klaviersatz konnte fast unverändert übernommen werden, hinzugefügt wurden lediglich Angaben zum Pedaleinsatz. Die Angabe *lunga corona* bedeutet, dass die Fermaten lang zu halten sind. Originaltonart E-Dur.

QUELLE: A. Dvořák, *Biblische Lieder*. Erstdruck, Simrock, Berlin 1895. – Englische Textfassung nach gebräuchlicher englischer Übersetzung des Psalm 23.

33.

Gabriel Fauré, *Cantique de Jean Racine* (Lobgesang des Jean Racine) Op. 11: Fauré schrieb das Werk 1865 für gemischten Chor mit Orgel- oder Klavierbegleitung (Des-Dur). Widmungsträger ist *Monsieur César Franck*. Neben dieser Originalfassung existiert auch eine Fassung für 2 Singstimmen (Sopran und Mezzosopran/Tenor) in D-Dur, welche als Vorlage für unsere Einrichtung für 1 Solostimme und Orgel diente. Im Begleitsatz wurden lediglich die tiefen Oktavverdopplungen, die nur mit Klavier ausführbar sind, weggelassen.

QUELLE: Ausgabe Hamelle, Paris 1903. – Deutsche Textfassung vom Herausgeber.

34.

Flor Peeters, *The Lord's Prayer*: Das Stück ist eine Vertonung des *Vater unser* in englischer Sprache. Der belgische Komponist Peeters genoss als Lehrer und weltweit tätiger Organist internationale Reputation. Ein auffallendes Merkmal seiner Tonsprache ist die Verwendung gregorianischer Melodien und modaler Skalen. – Der Begleitsatz von *The Lord's Prayer* ist gleichermaßen für Orgel oder für Klavier ausgelegt.

QUELLE: Ausgabe Edition Peters No. 6201c, New York 1961.

35.

Ralph Vaughan Williams, *The Call*: Bei diesem Lied handelt es sich um die Nr. 4 aus dem 1911 fertiggestellten Zyklus *Five Mystical Songs* nach Gedichten des englischen Mystikers George Herbert (1593–1633). Der originale Klaviersatz ist weitgehend auch auf der Orgel spielbar; Töne, die bei Ausführung auf der Orgel aus klanglichen Gründen besser wegbleiben, werden in kleinerem Stich wiedergegeben. Originaltonart Es-Dur.

QUELLE: R. Vaughan Williams, *Five Mystical Songs*. Galaxy Music Corporation, Boston. Der Abdruck erfolgt mit Genehmigung von Stainer & Bell, London.

36.

Jehan Alain, *Ave Maria*: Alain schrieb seine *Vocalise dorienne* im März 1937 für seine Schwester Marie-Odile (1914–1937) anlässlich eines dreitägigen gemeinsamen Aufenthaltes im Kloster Valloires. Die dortige Orgel war für den Komponisten ein gern gespieltes und inspirierendes Instrument. Das Stück wurde zu einem *in memoriam* für Marie-Odile, die wenig später bei einer Bergtour in den Alpen ums Leben kam.

Das für Gesang und Orgel (*chant et accomp. orgue*) komponierte Stück ist durch die Angabe *„Sur A"* (auf Vokal „A" zu singen) eindeutig ohne Textunterlegung konzipiert, was auch durch die weit gesetzten Legatobögen unterstrichen wird. (Eine Vorliebe zu textloser Vokalmusik zeigt sich bereits in Alains früherem Vokalwerk.) Im Manuskript ist in den ersten Takten in schwächerer Handschrift, offenbar von fremder Hand, der Versuch einer nachträglichen Textierung zu erkennen (*„Ave, verum corpus, natum de Maria virgine"*), nach einigen Takten abbrechend. Nach Alains frühem Tod (1940) unterlegte sein Vater Albert Alain (1880–1971) die Komposition mit dem Text des *Ave Maria*, wobei in der Gesangs- wie auch in der Orgelstimme eine Reihe von Modifikationen unumgänglich war. In dieser Fassung erschien das Werk 1996 im Druck und erfuhr weltweite Verbreitung.

Unsere Ausgabe gibt sowohl diese textierte als auch die ursprüngliche textlose Fassung (*Vocalise dorienne*) nach Jehan Alains Handschrift wieder. Lediglich in der Takteinteilung wurde auf die textierte Druckfassung zurückgegriffen und deren Notation im 2/1- und 3/1-Takt anstelle des ursprünglichen 2/2-Taktes übernommen.

Durch die beiden Fassungen bestehen – erstmals in einer Notenausgabe – folgende Möglichkeiten der Aufführung:

- nur die Fassung mit Textunterlegung, Takte 1–25
- nur die um einen Takt kürzere Urfassung (*Vocalise*)
- beide Fassungen nacheinander. Auch die umgekehrte Reihenfolge ist denkbar: zuerst *Vocalise*, danach *Ave Maria*.

Entsprechend Alains ursprünglicher Taktangabe *Alla breve* (¢) wird man die halben Noten als Grundschlag ansehen und, je nach Ausführbarkeit der Melodiephrasen, das Tempo zwischen 𝅗𝅥 = 60 und 80 wählen. Das Stück steht im Original eine kleine Terz höher.

QUELLE: J. Alain, *Œuvres vocales, Editions Musicales de la Schola Cantorum*, Fleurier (Schweiz) 1996.

37.

When I Have Sung My Songs to You ist das bekannteste Stück des amerikanischen Sängers und Komponisten Ernest Charles (1895–1984), der in seinen Liedern eine Verbindung zwischen amerikanisch geprägtem Songstil und ausdrucksvollem Kunstlied europäischer Tradition zu erreichen suchte. *When I Have Sung My Songs* entstand 1934 und wurde seither ins Repertoire vieler Sängerinnen und Sänger aufgenommen. Es ist ein schlichtes Liebeslied, das jedoch eine intensive Interpretation verlangt und sich vor allem als Zugabe am Ende eines Konzerts eignet. Originaltonart F-Dur.

QUELLE: Ausgabe G. Schirmer (Inc.), 1934

38.   

Amazing Grace (Traditional): Die heute weltweit bekannte pentatonische Melodie ist eine amerikanische Volksweise, die erstmals in einem Gesangbuch von 1831 namens *Virginia Harmony* auftauchte. Der Text stammt von dem amerikanischen Kapitän John Newton (1725–1807), der eine Zeit lang Sklavenhandel betrieben hatte. Nachdem er im Mai 1748 in schwere Seenot geraten und nach Anrufung der Gnade Gottes („Amazing Grace") gerettet worden war, behandelte er seine Sklaven menschlicher. So geläutert, zog er sich schließlich ganz aus diesem Metier zurück, wurde stattdessen Geistlicher und trat für die Bekämpfung der Sklaverei ein. In seiner Gedichtsammlung *Olney Hymns* (1779) ist der Text *„Amazing Grace"* als *Hymn 41* enthalten.
Die ursprüngliche, schlichtere Fassung der Melodie (ohne Triolen) ist in der 1. Strophe unseres Arrangements wiedergegeben. Die triolischen Bildungen (siehe 2.–4. Strophe) stammen aus späterer Zeit und sind vor allem durch prominente Interpreten wie Joan Baez, Judy Collins oder Jessye Norman zum Allgemeingut geworden.

39.

J. S. Bach, *Vergiss mein nicht* (BWV 505), ist eine der wenigen Melodien aus dem *Musicalischen Gesangbuch* von Georg Chr. Schemelli (1736), für die Bachs Autorschaft gesichert ist. Die Continuoaussetzung der 1. Strophe ist der Ausgabe von Eberhard Wenzel (Edition Peters Nr. 4612) entnommen, für die 2. Strophe wurde der Orgelsatz des Komponisten Robert Franz (1818–1892) gewählt. Originaltonart a-Moll.

QUELLE: *20 Sacred Songs, selected and arranged by Robert Franz.* Novello & Co. Ltd., London (19. Jhdt.), Platten-Nr. 7788. – Englische Textfassung von J. Troutbeck (1832–1899).

40.

J. S. Bach, *Schlummert ein, ihr matten Augen*: Diese Arie findet sich bereits im *Notenbuch für Anna Magdalena Bach* (1725), notiert für Singstimme und Continuo, Tonart G-Dur. Diese Fassung ist ohne Vor- und Zwischenspiele, sie diente als Grundlage für unsere Orgeleinrichtung. Um den zeitlichen Rahmen bei Feiern nicht zu überschreiten, wurde das Stück leicht gekürzt (Wegfall des Teiles *„Hier muss ich das Elend bauen"*). Das Nachspiel (ab T. 49 unserer Version) stammt aus Bachs eigener Bearbeitung dieser Arie, die er für Kantate Nr. 82 (*Ich habe genug*) anfertigte. Zu diesem Zweck hat der Komponist das Stück erweitert, für Basstimme umgeschrieben und um eine große Terz nach unten (Es-Dur) transponiert.

QUELLE: Neue Bach-Ausgabe *NBA* V/4. – Englische Textfassung nach Henry S. Drinker.

41.

Bist du bei mir findet sich in der bekannten Sammlung *Notenbüchlein der Anna Magdalena Bach* und wurde lange Zeit als Komposition J. S. Bachs angesehen (als BWV 508). Nach neueren Forschungen stammt die Melodie aber aus der 1718 aufgeführten Oper *Diomedes* von Gottfried Heinrich Stölzel und war in ihrer Zeit sehr verbreitet. Der Musikforscher Hermann Keller nannte *Bist du bei mir* „das vielleicht schönste Liebeslied des Barock". Aufgrund der im Text thematisierten Liebe bis zum Tod kann das Lied jedoch gleichermaßen einen musikalischen Beitrag bei Bestattungen darstellen. Der im Original lautende Text *„es drückten deine schönen Hände"* wurde hier, einer häufig gesungenen Praxis folgend, zu *„deine lieben Hände"* geändert. Originaltonart ist Es-Dur, eine Quarte höher. Continuoaussetzung vom Herausgeber.

QUELLE: *Notenbüchlein für Anna Magdalena Bach*, hrsg. von Hermann Keller, Edition Peters Nr. 4546. – Englische Textfassung von David Lewiston Sharpe.

42.

W. A. Mozart, *Ave verum*, KV 618: Diese Motette ist eine der bekanntesten Vertonungen des mittelalterlichen Textes. Mozart schrieb sie 1791 für das Fronleichnamsfest in Baden bei Wien. Heute wird sie häufig zur musikalischen Begleitung von Trauerfeiern eingesetzt. Die originale Instrumentation ist für gemischten Chor, Streicher und Orgel. Der Orgelsatz hier folgt Mozarts Streichersatz, die Singstimme entspricht der Sopranstimme des Chorsatzes.

QUELLE: Neue Mozart-Ausgabe I/3.

43.

Franz Schubert, *Im Abendrot*, D 799: In seiner (hier zugrunde gelegten) 2. Fassung hat Schubert dieses stimmungsvolle Lied mit *Langsam, feierlich* überschrieben. Es ist „Ausdruck einer Andacht, die sich der Vergänglichkeit des Lebensglückes ergreifend demütig bewußt wird" (D. Fischer-Dieskau). Geeignet für verschiedene Anlässe, besonders aber für Gedenkveranstaltungen und Trauerfeiern. Originaltonart As-Dur. Orgelbearbeitung vom Herausgeber, originaler Klaviersatz im Anhang, Seite 158.

QUELLE: Neue Schubert-Gesamtausgabe *NGA* IV/13 (2. Fassung von 1827).

44.

Franz Schubert, *Ins stille Land*, D 403: Das weithin unbekannte Lied bietet sich durch seinen Text gut zur Aufführung bei Trauerfeiern an. Der Name des Textdichters Johann Gaudenz von Salis-Seewis (1762–1834) ist vor allem noch durch das von J. Reichardt vertonte und bis heute gesungene Herbstlied *Bunt sind schon die Wälder* geläufig. Von *Ins stille Land* wurde hier die späteste der vier Fassungen ausgewählt. Bis auf eine klangliche Ausdünnung in den ersten drei Takten ist Schuberts Begleitsatz original wiedergegeben. Dietrich Fischer-Dieskau nennt das Lied „eine kleine Kostbarkeit, die verdiente bekannter zu sein" (*Auf den Spuren der Schubert-Lieder*).

QUELLE: Neue Schubert-Gesamtausgabe *NGA* IV/10.

45.

Felix Mendelssohn Bartholdy, *Sei stille dem Herrn*: Aufgrund der im Arientext angesprochenen christlichen Haltung, geprägt von Ergebenheit und Demut, eignet sich die bekannte Alt-Arie aus dem Oratoirum *Elias* besonders für Trauerfeierlichkeiten und Gedenkveranstaltungen verschiedener Art. Als Vorlage für die Erstellung des Orgelsatzes diente die Partitur.

QUELLE: F. Mendelssohn Bartholdy, *Elias*. Partitur und Klavierauszug, Edition Peters Nr. 11345 und 11346, Urtext, hrsg. von Klaus Burmeister, Frankfurt/M., 2011.

46. ✞

Robert Schumann, *Ruhe sanft in Gottes Frieden*: Das Schlusslied des Zyklus *Myrthen (Liederkreis für Gesang und Klavier)* Op. 25, komponiert auf einen Text von Friedrich Rückert (*„Hier in diesen erdbeklommnen Lüften“*), erfuhr Ende des 19. Jahrhunderts die hier wiedergegebene, ganz auf Traueranlässe zugeschnittene Umtextierung des Komponisten und Literaten Theobald Rehbaum (1835–1918). Originaltonart As-Dur.

QUELLE: *Hosianna, Ausgewählte geistliche Lieder und Arien*, Robert Lienau Musikverlag, Nr. RL 19590.

47. ✞

Wilhelm Berger ist im heutigen Konzertleben weitgehend unbekannt, er darf dennoch als herausragende kompositorische Begabung angesehen werden. Sein musikalisches Œuvre ist vielschichtig und steht, zeitlich wie stilistisch, zwischen Brahms und Reger. Das hier ausgewählte Lied *Selig sind des Himmels Erben* Op. 49/2 zeichnet sich durch modale Wendungen aus. Der Text stammt von Friedrich Gottlieb Klopstock (1724–1803) und findet sich in dessen Sammlung *Geistliche Lieder* im Abschnitt *Vorbereitung zum Tode*. Originaltonart c-Moll (mit zwei ♭-Vorzeichen).

QUELLE: W. Berger, *Zwei geistliche Lieder* Op. 49 für hohe Singstimme mit Harmonium (oder Orgel), Verlag Carl Simon, Berlin 1899. Die Vorlage, in der auch die englische Textfassung enthalten ist, wurde uns freundlicherweise von den Meininger Museen zur Verfügung gestellt, wo ein umfangreicher Teilnachlass Bergers aufbewahrt wird.

48. ✞

Max Reger, *Bitte um einen seligen Tod*: 1914 komponierte Reger seine *12 geistlichen Lieder* Op. 137 (*Fräulein M. Wach gewidmet*). Das hier ausgewählte erste Stück, ein choralhafter, harmonisch sehr farbiger Satz, kann gleichermaßen auf Klavier, Harmonium oder Orgel gespielt werden. Der Textdichter Nikolaus Herman (ca. 1480–1561) war Kantor und Pfarrer und trat auch als Verfasser evangelischer Kirchenlieder hervor.

QUELLE: M. Reger, *Zwölf geistliche Lieder*, Edition Peters Nr. 3452. – Englische Textfassung von Jean Lunn, Edition Peters Nr. 6832, C. F. Peters Corporation, New York 1964.

49. ✞

Gabriel Fauré, *Pie Jesu*: Für sein bekanntestes Werk, das *Requiem* Op. 48, komponierte Fauré dieses „überirdisch“ schöne Stück für Sopran, Orgel und Orchester. Es eignet sich, besonders bei schlichter, undramatischer Vortragsweise, gut für Trauerfeiern. Im hier vorliegenden Begleitsatz für Orgel allein wurden die solistischen Orgelpassagen des Originals beibehalten. Originaltonart B-Dur.

QUELLE: G. Fauré, *Requiem*. Partitur, Urtext, hrsg. von R. Zimmermann und J. Nectoux, Edition Peters Nr. 9563.

50. 🎂 ✞

Hugo Wolf, *Gebet* (*„Herr, schicke was du willt“*): Das 1888 nach einem Text Eduard Mörikes komponierte Lied hat im Klaviersatz schon einen orgelmäßigen Duktus. Max Reger übertrug es 1898 für Singstimme und Orgel. Diese Fassung wie auch die Originalversion mit Klavier sind in der vorliegenden Sammlung enthalten. Klaviersatz im Anhang, S. 160.

QUELLE: H. Wolf, *Geistliche Lieder*, für eine Singstimme und Orgel bearbeitet von Max Reger, Edition Peters Nr. 3231. – Englische Textfassung von John Bernhoff (19. Jhdt).

Notes on the individual pieces

1.

Heinrich Schütz, *Bringt her dem Herren / Bring to the Lord God* (SWV 283) is the first of the *Kleine geistliche Konzerte* (Short Sacred Concertos) written for voice and continuo. Owing to its lively style, this piece lends itself to a range of different occasions, in particular those in a church, and is especially well suited to the opening of a ceremony. Continuo realization by the editor. Original key C major.

SOURCE: Alte Schütz-Gesamtausgabe (1887) and the edition edited by Wilhelm Ehmann and Hans Hoffmann, Kassel 1963. – English version of the text by Jean Lunn (Schütz, *Five Short Sacred Concertos for Voice and Organ*, Edition Peters No. 6894, New York 1966).

2.

J. S. Bach, *Wachet auf, ruft uns die Stimme / Zion hears the watchman* is a movement from Cantata No. 140 of the same name, originally for tenor, strings (with unison violins and violas in the upper part) and basso continuo. Here, Bach combines the choral melody with a melodically expressive accompaniment featuring a pithy opening theme. Bach's arrangement of this piece for solo organ (BWV 645) has also been taken into consideration. The notes in small print in this version should be omitted when performing on the organ. Original key E flat major.

SOURCE: Vocal score, Edition Breitkopf; Neue Bach-Ausgabe *NBA* I/27. – English version of the text by Charles Sanford Terry (1864–1936).

3.

J. S. Bach, *Bekennen will ich seinen Namen* (BWV 200) comes down to us as a single aria and should probably be regarded as a fragment of a sacred cantata that no longer survives. This beautiful alto aria, which can be sung equally well by a mezzo-soprano or bright baritone voice, dates from Bach's final creative period and was only discovered and published some 200 years after it was composed. The piano part has been arranged by the editor of the present collection from Bach's score for two violins and basso continuo. The two violins and the bass line are indicated in normal print and the harmonic fills in small print.

SOURCE: J. S. Bach, *Bekennen will ich seinen Namen*. Full score and parts, edited by Ludwig Landshoff, Leipzig 1935, Edition Peters No. 4209.

4.

J. S. Bach, *Schafe können sicher weiden / Sheep May Safely Graze*, from the "Hunting Cantata", BWV 208. As in No. 2 (*Wachet auf*), Bach has underlaid the solo voice with a characteristic accompaniment whose principal theme is perhaps more memorable than the vocal part. In bars 30–40 the German text has been altered. The original German words of the secular cantata in this passage are: *"Wo Regenten wohl regieren, kann man Ruh' und Frieden spüren, und was Länder glücklich macht."* Original instrumentation: soprano, two recorders and continuo. This arrangement reproduces the two recorder parts in normal print; the small notes may be left out for ease of playing. Passages accompanied in the original by continuo alone are indicated throughout in small print in the RH. Original key B flat major.

SOURCE: Neue Bach-Ausgabe *NBA* I/35. – English version of the text by the editor based on Charles Sanford Terry (1864–1936).

5.

G. F. Handel, *He Shall Feed His Flock / Er weidet seine Herde* This famous soprano aria from the *Messiah* can be used to create an atmospheric highlight at a number of different occasions. Because of the steady tempo of the piece, the organ is to be preferred as accompanying instrument. There is a variant of the aria by Handel himself which begins in F major (alto voice) and returns to the original key of B flat major (soprano) at *"Kommt her zu ihm" / "Come unto Him"*. In the here given arrangement the alto register is retained throughout. As the original performance time of approx. 8 minutes is often felt to be too long, the repeats written out by the composer have been cut (20 bars in total). Organ arrangement by the editor. Piano part provided on page 150 (Appendix).

SOURCE: G. F. Handel, *Messiah*, edited by Donald Burrows, Edition Peters No. 7317. German version by Julius Stern (Edition Peters No. 60).

6.

G. F. Handel, *Where e'er You Walk* is taken from Act II of the oratorio *Semele*, HWV 58. Due to the nature of its text, this aria lends itself well to wedding ceremonies. The organ part is based on Handel's string parts. Original key B flat major.

SOURCE: G. F. Handel, *Semele*, Vol. 7, F. Chrysander edition, 1860.

7.

G. F. Handel, *Verdi prati, selve amene* is an aria for mezzo-soprano from Handel's Italian opera *Alcina* (HWV 34), composed in 1735. The corresponding role (Ruggiero) was originally sung by a male voice (castrato). The aria concerns the fading beauty of nature and testifies to Handel's ability to make an intense statement with modest musical means. Thanks to its expressive simplicity, the piece can be sung at a wide variety of occasions. The accompaniment is based on Handel's original scoring (violins I/II, viola, continuo). The notes in small print are designed to fill out the piano sound. The small notes in brackets can be played on the pedals when accompanying on the organ. English text by Nathan Haskiel Dole (1852–1935).

SOURCE: G. F. Handel, *Alcina*, F. Chrysander edition, Vol. 86, 1868. – English version of the text based on the edition for voice and piano by Ebenezer Prout, Oliver Ditson Company, 1905.

8.

Giuseppe Giordani, *Caro mio ben*. This love song achieved great popularity as long ago as the 18th century, thanks in part to the performances given by castrato Gasparo Pacchierotti in London in 1778. The work is sometimes attributed to Giordani's brother Tommaso (c. 1730–1806). The ornamentation suggestions in bars 19, 22, 29 and 30 (small notes) are the editor's. Original key F major.

SOURCE: *A Selection of Italian Arias 1600–1800*, Vol. I, edited by Anthony Lewis, High Voice, ABRSM 1983.

9.

L. van Beethoven, *All Nature Sings God's Praises* (*"Die Himmel rühmen"*) is the fourth of the *Six Gellert Songs* Op. 48. This song, of which there are several arrangements for choir, extols the greatness of God's creation and can be sung at a number of different occasions. It is a favourite of many solo tenors. Organ arrangement by the editor. Original key C major. Piano part provided on page 153 (Appendix).

SOURCE: L. v. Beethoven, *Ausgewählte Lieder*, Edition Peters No. 180 (with additional verses) and Neue Beethoven Gesamtausgabe XII/1. – English version of the text by Frederick Fuller from: *The Art of Song*. Grades 1–5. Edition Peters No. 7441, London 1994.

10.

L. van Beethoven, *I Love Thee As Thou Lovest Me* (*"Tender Love"*), WoO 123. A modest but timeless love song composed by the 27-year-old Beethoven, this piece is popular as a serenade at weddings as well as silver/golden wedding anniversaries. The text is by Karl Friedrich Wilhelm Herrosee (1754–1823), a preacher and church dean and the author of various hymn texts. Beethoven did not include any dynamic markings in the autograph; those in the present version, taken from later editions, are therefore to be regarded as suggestions only. The original piano part has been provided by way of accompaniment. When performing on the organ, the lower octave in octave passages should be omitted and the two closing chords thinned out. Original key G major.

SOURCE: L. v. Beethoven, *Ausgewählte Lieder*, Edition Peters No. 180 (with additional verses) and Neue Beethoven Gesamtausgabe XII/1. – English version from a single edition published by J. André, Offenbach (c. 1870).

11.

Felix Mendelssohn Bartholdy, *O for the Wings of a Dove* WoO 15 (work number B 49 in the New Leipzig Edition). *Hear My Prayer*, for solo soprano, mixed choir and organ is based on texts from Psalm 55, compiled for Mendelssohn by the Englishman William Bartholomew (1793–1867). The piece is particularly popular in the English-speaking world.

This is an abridged version, consisting of the opening of *Hear My Prayer* and the whole of the lyrical section *O for the Wings of a Dove*, with the upper voice taken over from the choral part. The organ follows Mendelssohn's original organ accompaniment. For the sake of general suitability, the words *"In die Wüste eilt ich dann fort"* have been changed to *„Auf den Flügeln eilt ich dann fort"*. Original key G major.

SOURCE: Breitkopf & Härtel, Leipzig 1875. – English text version from: Mendelssohn, *Hear my Prayer. The Choralist*, No. 300, Boosey & Co. (c. 1896).

12.

Robert Schumann, *Widmung / Devotion* (*"Du meine Seele"*). This piece, which opens the song cycle *Myrthen* Op. 25, was presented by Schumann to his bride Clara as a gift on their wedding day (12 September 1840). It has remained one of the best-known love songs of the Romantic period ever since. The text is by Friedrich Rückert. Arrangement of the piano part for organ by the editor. Original key A flat major.

SOURCE: R. Schumann, *Lieder*, Vol. I, edited by Max Friedländer, Edition Peters No. 2383b. – English version of the text by the editor in collaboration with Denette Whitter.

13.

Robert Schumann, *Du Ring an meinem Finger*. As a symbol of marriage, this song occupies a special place in the cycle *Frauenliebe und Leben* Op. 42. The piano part has been adopted for the organ with only a few changes (in bars 25–30, for example, the repeated notes in the LH have been replaced by sustained notes). Text: Adelbert von Chamisso.

SOURCE: R. Schumann, *Frauenliebe und Leben*, Urtext, edited by H. J. Köhler, Edition Peters No. 9536. – English version of the text by Lewis Novra and Louis Charles Elson, from: *Schumann Album, 40 ausgewählte Lieder*, Braunschweig 1887 (Collection Litolff No. 1691).

14.

Louis Roessel, *Kavatine* (*"Wenn ich mit Menschen- und mit Engelzungen"*). Although Roessel is sadly neglected as a composer today, his opus 25 (subtitle *Trauungsgesang*, or Wedding Song) continues to be performed regularly at ceremonies in the German-speaking world, not least due to its highly expressive text, which is taken from the New Testament, I. Corinthians chapter 13, verses 1–3, 12–13. The organ accompaniment was adapted from the original piano part. Original key G major.

SOURCE: *Hosianna, Ausgewählte geistliche Lieder und Arien*, Lienau Verlag, No. 124.

15.

Eugen Hildach, *Wo du hingehst / Where'er Thou Goest*. This song is based on an excerpt from the Old Testament (the Book of Ruth) which has been set many times (see also songs 18 and 19) and is very popular at weddings and wedding anniversaries. Hildach was a singing teacher at the conservatory in Breslau (present-day Wrocław) and himself a concert singer. With his wife Anna, a mezzo-soprano, he organised lieder evenings and oratorio performances. *Wo du hingehst* has remained his best-known song to this day. The first edition has both piano and separate organ accompaniment and provides the organ part and English text (by John Bernhoff) for this version. Text: Old Testament, Book of Ruth, chapter 1, verses 16–17. Original key D major.

SOURCE: First edition, Heinrichshofen's Verlag, Magdeburg 1898.

16.

Edvard Grieg, *Ich liebe dich / I Love but Thee*. This famous love song is the third of the *Melodies of the Heart* Op. 5, with texts by Hans Christian Andersen. In addition to the Danish words, the first edition also included a rendering into German by Franz von Holstein which is still widely used today. In the piano accompaniment, which does not lend itself well to performance on the organ, various notes that are difficult to reach have been set inside brackets. They can be omitted for ease of playing.

SOURCE: *Edvard Grieg Complete Edition*, Vol. 14, from which the English text by W. H. Halverson (adapted slightly) is also taken.

17.

Guy d' Hardelot, *Because*. This song for voice and piano, composed in the style of a show tune, is very popular in the English-speaking world. Guy d' Hardelot (real name: Helen Rhodes) was born to a French mother and an English father and entered the Paris Conservatoire at the age of 15. She subsequently worked in London as a singing teacher and also became successful as a composer of songs. The original French text of *Because* is by the author herself but the song was to achieve international popularity mainly in the English translation by Edward Teschemacher. The notes in small print in the voice part are alternatives suggested by the editor. This piece is best accompanied by piano/keyboard rather than organ. The first edition contains numerous pedal markings that have not been retained. Original key C major.

Source: Chappell & Co. edition, 1900, No. 21782.

18.

Paul Dessau, *Entreat Me Not*. This song was written in Hollywood in 1945 for the wedding of the composer's daughter Eva. Dessau took the English text from the Book of Ruth in the Old Testament (chapter 1, verses 16–17).

Source: P. Dessau, *Lieder aus dem Nachlass*, Urtext, edited by Axel Bauni, Edition Peters No. 11098, Frankfurt/Main 2009.

19.

Flor Peeters, *Wedding Song*. Of this song, which exists in both solo and choral versions (each with piano or organ accompaniment), the editor of the first edition (1962) wrote: "Compositions of this type enable us to convert weddings which otherwise are merely pretty into weddings which are truly beautiful." Text: Book of Ruth in the Old Testament (chapter 1, verses 16–17). Adaption of the English text by Hugh Ross.

Source: Fl. Peeters, *Wedding Song, edited by Walter E. Buszin*, C. F. Peters Corporation No. 6244c, New York 1962.

20.

Alan Hovhaness, *Love's Philosophy*. Hovhaness, an American composer of Armenian descent, is one of America's most-performed composers. Stylistically, his work borrows from both Armenian and European (specifically Renaissance) traditions. It also reveals other influences, such as Post-romanticism and Indian music. Hovhaness wrote *Love's Philosophy*, his opus 370, in 1984 for the wedding of two of his friends. The text is by the English poet Percy Bysshe Shelley (1792–1822). The original key is A minor, a fourth higher.

Source: Edition Peters No. 67522, C. F. Peters Corporation, New York 1994.

21.

Stefan Nilsson, *Fly With Me (Lenas sång)*. This song is featured in the Swedish film *As it is in Heaven*. Since its publication in 2004, a wide range of singers, including pop musicians, have made it their own. Stefan Nilsson made a name for himself primarily with his film scores but has also composed in other genres, such as ballet and opera.

Source: Single edition for solo voice and piano, Gehrmans Musikförlag, No. 10814. Reproduced by kind permission of the publisher.

22.

J. S. Bach, *Jesu, Joy of Man's Desiring* (from Cantata No. 147). This well-known chorale with its characteristic triplet accompaniment exists in numerous arrangements, many of them purely instrumental. It is one of the "universal" pieces in this collection – in other words, those that can be performed at both joyful and sorrowful occasions. Bach scored the work for four-part mixed choir, strings, oboe (doubling violin I), trumpet (doubling the soprano voice) and continuo. In this arrangement for voice and organ, the solo voice takes the soprano line and – as far as possible – the original string part. The notes in small print are intended for performance on the piano but may be omitted for ease of playing. Original key G major.

Source: Neue Bach-Ausgabe *NBA* I/28. – English version of the text by Charles Sanford Terry (1864–1936).

23.

Bach-Gounod, *Ave Maria*. In 1852 the French opera composer Charles Gounod wrote a *"Mélodie religieuse"* over the first prelude of J. S. Bach's *Well-tempered Clavier Book I*. It achieved worldwide popularity and lends itself to performance at virtually any occasion. Although the first edition contains a dedication to the French opera singer Mme. Miolan-Carvalho, the piece is also suitable for tenor voice. In the original G major version, Gounod sets bars 20–38 in a very low register; in this edition these notes have been raised by an octave. The alternative text printed in italics from bar 24 onwards is intended primarily for use in Protestant contexts.

Source: J. S. Bach / C. Gounod, *Ave Maria*. Edition in three keys (G major, F major and D major), Urtext, edited by Roger Nichols, Edition Peters No. 7668.

24.

Antonio Vivaldi, *Domine Deus*. This movement (from the ten-movement *Gloria*, RV 589) is another work that has proved popular at a range of different occasions. Vivaldi scored the piece for soprano, solo oboe (or violin) and continuo. In the accompaniment provided here, the small notes are harmonic fills in the manner of a continuo realization. Original key C major.

Source: A. Vivaldi, *Gloria*. Full score and vocal score, Urtext, edited by Klaus Burmeister, Edition Peters Nos. 8866 and 8867.

25.

G. F. Handel, *"Largo"* (*Ombra mai fù*) from the opera *Xerxes* (orig. *Serse*, HWV 40). This short aria, which opens the opera, extols the virtues of a pleasant shady spot beneath a plane tree and is one of Handel's most popular pieces. There has been no shortage of attempts to substitute different words, in other languages too, but none of the alternatives has gained any great currency. If necessary, the original Italian words can be replaced by the later text provided here as a second verse (*"Tu sei il mio ciel"*). In order to make a more substantial performance piece for important occasions, both verses can, of course, be sung. The organ accompaniment generally follows the original string parts: the left hand covers the bass part and some of the lower notes of the middle register while the right hand covers the two upper parts. Original key F major.

Source: G. F. Handel, *Serse*. Chrysander edition, Vol. 92, Leipzig 1884.

26. 

L. van Beethoven, *Bitten* (*"Gott, deine Güte reicht so weit"* / *"To Thee, My God"*). Beethoven composed his *Six Songs* Op. 48 on texts by Christian Fürchtegott Gellert (1715–1769) in 1803 and dedicated them to Count Johann Georg von Browne on the occasion of the death of his wife Anna Margarete. The original piano part already displays organ-like characteristics and has therefore been retained for the most part for performance on the organ. Original key E major.
Source: L. v. Beethoven, *Ausgewählte Lieder*, Edition Peters No. 180 (with additional verses) and Neue Beethoven-Gesamtausgabe XII/1. – English version of the text from a historical edition (19th century).

27.

Franz Schubert, *Ave Maria*, D 839. In 1825, Schubert set several excerpts from the epic poem *The Lady of the Lake* by the Scottish poet Sir Walter Scott (1771–1832) in a German translation by D. Adam Storck. This song was originally entitled *Ellen's Gesang III* / *Hymne an die Jungfrau* (Ellen's Third Song / Prayer to the Virgin Mary). In Scott's poem, Ellen, the daughter of the Earl of Douglas, flees to the wilderness to escape the attentions of an unloved suitor, Roderick. One evening, Roderick hears her song, accompanied on the harp, drifting across the lake and is uncertain whether it is Ellen or an angel singing. The piano part has been arranged as a simple trio-like accompaniment for the organ. Notes in small print are intended for performance on organs with two manuals. The original piano part is provided on p. 155 of the Appendix.
Source: F. Schubert, *Lieder*, new edition by Dietrich Fischer-Dieskau and Elmar Budde, Vol. III, edition for medium voice, Edition Peters No. 8305b (three verses).

28.

Ferdinand Hiller, *Gebet* / *Prayer* (*"Be Near Me Still"*) Op. 46 No. 1. Hiller was a friend of Mendelssohn and Schumann and a pivotal figure in the Rhenish musical life of his day. It is chiefly *Gebet* that has kept his memory alive, wherein the text by Emanuel Geibel (1815–1884), constituting a profession of faith and an expression of trust, has played an important part. The song is particularly well suited to confirmations and other religious occasions. The piano and organ accompaniments are the composer's own. Original key F major.
Source: *Hosianna, Ausgewählte geistliche Lieder und Arien*, Lienau-Verlag. – English version of the text by Alma Strettell (19th century).

29.

César Franck, *Panis angelicus*. Franck wrote this famous piece in 1872 and added it retrospectively to his *Messe à trois voix* Op. 12, written 12 years before. *Panis angelicus* ("The Angelic Bread") was originally scored for solo voice, organ, harp and violoncello. In the present accompaniment for organ alone the cello voice has been transposed an octave higher and some of the harp part conveyed by staccato notes. – The composer took his text from the sixth verse of St Thomas Aquinas's hymn for the feast of Corpus Christus, the *Sacris Solemnis* (13th century). In English, the meaning of the text is as follows: "The angelic bread has become the bread of man. The bread of heaven vanquisheth earthly spectres. O wonder! The poor and humble servant taketh unto himself the Lord." Original key A major.
Source: C. Franck, *Messe à trois voix*. Full score, first edition, E. Repos / Bornemann, Paris 1872.

30.

Anton Bruckner, *Ave Maria*. With its characteristic modulations, this 1882 setting of the prayer to the Virgin exemplifies the composer's mature style. Bruckner dedicated the work to *Fräulein Luise Hochleitner*, the sister-in-law of his pupil Camillo Horn. The accompaniment follows Bruckner's original (for "piano, organ or harmonium"), albeit with the parts redistributed for performance on an instrument with pedal board. The notes in small print in the voice part (bars 72–74) are editorial suggestions.
Source: A. Bruckner, *Kleine Kirchenmusikwerke 1835–1892*, Musikwissenschaftlicher Verlag der Internationalen Bruckner-Gesellschaft, Vienna 1984 (Kritische Gesamtausgabe, Vol. 21).

31.

Camille Saint-Saëns, *Deus Abraham*. This work was composed in 1885 and is scored for soprano, mixed choir, organ and ad libitum harp. This arrangement for voice and organ is the editor's. In bars 21–32 the upper voice of the choral setting has been followed. Original key F major.
Source: First edition, Durand, Paris 1892.

32.

Antonín Dvořák, *The Lord is My Shepherd*. This is the fourth of the *Biblical Songs* Op. 99, composed in 1894 to the words of Psalm 23. Dvořák's setting takes the form of a monodic appeal, with a spare accompaniment that gives the solo voice plenty of freedom. The piano part has been adopted almost unchanged, with some pedal markings added. The *lunga corona* marking indicates that the fermatas are to be prolonged. Original key E major.
Source: A. Dvořák, *Biblische Lieder*. First edition, Simrock, Berlin 1895. – English version of the text based on a common English translation of Psalm 23.

33.

Gabriel Fauré, *Cantique de Jean Racine* (Canticle of Jean Racine) Op. 11. Fauré wrote this work for mixed choir with organ or piano accompaniment in 1865. It is dedicated to *Monsieur César Franck*. In addition to the original version in D flat there is another for two voices (soprano and mezzo-soprano/tenor) in D major, on which the present arrangement for solo voice and organ is based. The omission of the low octave doubling, which is playable only on the piano, is the only change to the accompaniment.
Source: Hamelle edition, Paris 1903. – German version of the text by the editor.

34.

Flor Peeters, *The Lord's Prayer*. The Belgian composer Flor Peeters enjoyed an international reputation as a teacher and organist and, as a performer, was in demand all over the world. A conspicuous feature of his musical language is the use of Gregorian melodies and modal scales. The accompaniment to *The Lord's Prayer* is arranged for organ or piano.
Source: Edition Peters No. 6201c, New York 1961.

35.

Ralph Vaughan Williams, *The Call*. This song is the fourth in the cycle *Five Mystical Songs*, settings of poems by the English mystic George Herbert (1593–1633), completed in 1911. The original piano accompaniment is also playable for the most part on the organ; notes that are better left out when performing on the organ are given in small print. Original key E flat major.

Source: R. Vaughan Williams, *Five Mystical Songs*. Galaxy Music Corporation, Boston. Reproduced by permission of Stainer & Bell, London.

36.

Jehan Alain, *Ave Maria*. Alain wrote his *Vocalise dorienne* for his sister Marie-Odile (1914–1937) during their three-day visit to the Abbaye de Valloires (where the organ was a source of considerable inspiration to him) in March 1937: the piece was to become a memorial to Marie-Odile, who died shortly afterwards while mountaineering in the Alps.

Composed for voice and organ (*chant et accomp. orgue*), the piece bears the instruction *"Sur A"* (i.e. to be sung on the vowel "A") and thus was clearly conceived without text: this is further emphasized by the long slurs (a predilection for vocal music without text is already apparent in Alain's earlier vocal works). In the manuscript, the words *"Ave, verum corpus, natum de Maria virgine"* can be made out in a fainter, later hand, but this attempt to furnish the song with a text breaks off after just a few bars. After Alain's premature death in 1940, his father Albert Alain (1880–1971) added the text of the *Ave Maria*, necessitating a series of modifications to both the voice and organ parts. His version was published in 1996 and achieved worldwide fame.

The present edition offers both versions (with and without text), and is based on Jehan Alain's autograph (although the 2/1 and 3/1 notation of the published version has been adopted in place of the composer's original 2/2).

For the first time in a published edition, presentation of the two versions together offers the following performance possibilities:

- only the version with text, bars 1–25
- only the original version (*Vocalise*), which has been shortened by one bar
- the two versions in succession, either as presented here or in reverse (the *Vocalise* followed by *Ave Maria*.

Corresponding to Alain's original *alla breve* (¢) time signature, the minims are to be regarded as the basic pulse and a tempo of between 𝅗𝅥 = 60 and 80 is recommended. The original version of the piece is a minor third higher.

Source: J. Alain, *Œuvres vocales, Editions Musicales de la Schola Cantorum*, Fleurier (Switzerland) 1996.

37.

When I Have Sung My Songs to You is the best-known work by American singer and composer Ernest Charles (1895–1984), who sought to unite the American style of songwriting with the expressive European tradition of the Lied. *When I have Sung My Songs* was composed in 1934 and has enjoyed a place in the repertoire of many singers, both male and female, ever since. It is a simple love song that nevertheless calls for a certain intensity of interpretation. It is especially suitable as an encore for the end of a concert. Original key F major.

Source: G. Schirmer edition (Inc.), 1934

38.

Amazing Grace (traditional). This world-famous pentatonic melody was originally an American folk tune that appeared for the first time in a songbook of 1831 entitled *Virginia Harmony*. The text was written by an American sea captain John Newton (1725–1807), who had been active in the slave trade. In May 1748 he got into severe distress at sea and was rescued after calling upon God's grace, whereupon he began to treat his slaves more humanely. Thus reformed, he finally withdrew from the slave trade altogether, became a clergyman and campaigned for the abolition of slavery. *Amazing Grace* was included as no. 41 in his collection *Olney Hymns* (1779). The original, simpler version (without triplets) is reproduced in the first verse of the present arrangement. The triplets (verses 2–4) date from a later period and became common thanks to prominent interpretations of the song by the likes of Joan Baez, Judy Collins and Jessye Norman.

39.

J. S. Bach, *Vergiss mein nicht / Forget Me Not* (BWV 505) is one of the few melodies from Georg Christian Schemelli's *Musicalisches Gesangbuch* (1736) for which Bach's authorship has been firmly established. The continuo realization of the first verse is taken from the Eberhard Wenzel edition (Edition Peters No. 4612); for the second verse the organ part by the composer Robert Franz (1818–1892) has been used. Original key A minor.

Source: *20 Sacred Songs, selected and arranged by Robert Franz*. Novello & Co. Ltd., London (19th century), plate no. 7788. – English version of the text by J. Troutbeck (1832–1899).

40.

J. S. Bach, *Schlummert ein, ihr matten Augen / Close Ye Now, Ye Weary Eyelids*. This aria first appeared in the *Notebook for Anna Magdalena Bach* (1725), scored for voice and continuo in the key of G major. This early version is without the prelude and interludes (which subsequently appeared in Cantata No. 82 – *Ich habe genug*) and serves as the basis for the organ arrangement in this edition. The piece has been abridged slightly through the omission of the passage *"Hier muss ich das Elend bauen"*. The postlude (from bar 49 onwards in this version) is taken from Bach's own arrangement for the cantata (where the piece is transposed down a major third, to E flat major, for bass voice).

Source: Neue Bach-Ausgabe *NBA* V/4. – English version of the text based on Henry S. Drinker.

41.

Bist du bei mir / With Thou Beside is found in the well-known collection *Notebook for Anna Magdalena Bach* and was long attributed to J. S. Bach (as BWV 508). Recent research, however, has discovered that the melody derives from the opera *Diomedes* by Gottfried Heinrich Stölzel and achieved considerable popularity in its day. The musicologist Hermann Keller has described *Bist du bei mir* as "perhaps the most beautiful love song of the Baroque age". In view of its theme of a love that endures unto death, the song also lends itself to being performed at funerals. In keeping with normal singing practice, the line *"es drückten deine schönen Hände"* ("were your fair hands [to close my eyes]") has been changed to *"deine lieben Hände"* ("your dear hands"). Original key E flat major, a fourth higher. Continuo realisation by the editor.

Source: *Notebook for Anna Magdalena Bach*, edited by Hermann Keller, Edition Peters No. 4546. – English version of the text by David Lewiston Sharpe.

42.

W. A. Mozart, *Ave verum*, K 618. This motet is one of the best-known settings of the medieval Ave veum text. It was composed by Mozart in 1791 for the feast of Corpus Christi in Baden, near Vienna. Today it is often performed at funeral ceremonies. It was originally scored for mixed choir, strings and organ. In this version, the organ accompaniment follows Mozart's scoring for strings, while the voice corresponds to the soprano line of the choral part.

Source: Neue Mozart-Ausgabe I/3.

43.

Franz Schubert, *Im Abendrot / Evening Glow*, D 799. In its second version (which serves as the basis for the present edition), Schubert gave this atmospheric song the marking: *Slowly, solemnly*. It is the "expression of a devotion that is movingly aware of the transitory nature of life's happiness" (D. Fischer-Dieskau, *Schubert: A Biographical Study of his Songs*). The piece is suitable for a number of different occasions, especially memorial and funeral services. Original key A flat major. Organ arrangement by the editor. Original piano part provided on page 158 (Appendix).

Source: Neue Schubert-Gesamtausgabe IV/13 (second version, 1827).

44.

Franz Schubert, *Ins stille Land*, D 403. Due to the nature of its text, this largely unknown song lends itself well to performance at funerals. The poet, Johann Gaudenz von Salis-Seewis (1762–1834), is known mainly by the setting by J. Reichardt of the autumn song *Bunt sind schon die Wälder*, which is still sung today. There are four versions of *Ins stille Land*: this edition is based on the last. Other than a thinning out of the sonorities in the first three bars, Schubert's original accompaniment has been retained. Dietrich Fischer-Dieskau describes this song "as a little gem that deserves to be better known" (*Schubert: A Biographical Study of his Songs*).

Source: Neue Schubert-Ausgabe *NGA* IV/10.

45.

Felix Mendelssohn Bartholdy, *Sei stille dem Herrn / O Rest in The Lord*. Because of the Christian devotion and humility expressed in it, this well-known alto aria from the oratorio *Elijah* is particularly well suited to performance at funerals and memorial services. The organ accompaniment is based on the full score.

Source: F. Mendelssohn Bartholdy, *Elijah*. Full score and vocal score, Edition Peters Nos. 11345 and 11346, Urtext, edited by Klaus Burmeister, Frankfurt/Main, 2011.

46.

Robert Schumann, *Ruhe sanft in Gottes Frieden*. The closing song in the cycle Myrthen Op. 25, this setting for voice and piano of a text by Friedrich Rückert (*"Hier in diesen erdbeklommnen Lüften"*), was subsequently furnished with a new text by the composer and writer Theobald Rehbaum (1835–1918). This later version, reproduced here, is suitable for performance at funerals and memorial services. Original key A flat major.

Source: *Hosianna, Ausgewählte geistliche Lieder und Arien*, Robert Lienau Musikverlag, No. RL 19590.

47.

Wilhelm Berger, *Selig sind des Himmels Erben / Blessed are the Heirs of Heaven*. Although largely unknown to today's concert audiences, Wilhelm Berger deserves to be recognized as an outstandingly talented composer. His musical oeuvre is multilayered and stands – both chronologically and stylistically – between Brahms and Reger. *Selig sind des Himmels Erben*, Op. 49/2, is unusual for its major/minor switches. The text is by Friedrich Gottlieb Klopstock (1724–1803) and is taken from the *Preparation for Death* section of the poet's collection *Geistliche Lieder* (Spiritual Songs). Original key C minor (with two ♭-accidentals).

Source: W. Berger, *Zwei geistliche Lieder* Op. 49 for high voice and harmonium (or organ), Verlag Carl Simon, Berlin 1899. The original, which also contains the English version of the text, was kindly made available to us by Meiningen Museums (Germany), which hold a substantial portion of Berger's archive.

48.

Max Reger, *Bitte um einen seligen Tod / Prayer for a Blessed Death*. Reger composed his *12 geistliche Lieder* Op. 137 (dedicated to *Fräulein M. Wach*) in 1914. The first, which has been selected for the present collection, is a chorale-like, harmonically highly colourful piece that can be played on the piano, harmonium or organ. Nikolaus Herman (c. 1480–1561), the author of the text, was a choirmaster/organist and pastor and is known to have written a number of Protestant hymns.

Source: M. Reger, *Zwölf geistliche Lieder*, Edition Peters No. 3452. – English version of the text by Jean Lunn, Edition Peters No. 6832, C. F. Peters Corporation, New York 1964.

49.

Gabriel Fauré, *Pie Jesu*. This piece of ethereal beauty, originally scored for soprano, organ and orchestra, was composed by Fauré for his best-known work, the *Requiem* Op. 48. When performed in a simple, undramatic manner, it is well suited to performance at funeral ceremonies. The accompaniment to this version, for organ alone, retains the soloistic organ passages of the original. Original key B flat major.

Source: G. Fauré, *Requiem*. Full score, Urtext, edited by R. Zimmermann and J. Nectoux, Edition Peters No. 9563.

50.

Hugo Wolf, *Gebet ("Herr, schicke, was du willt")* / Prayer (*"Lord, Send What Thou Deem'st Best"*). The piano part of this 1888 setting of a text by Eduard Mörike is already very organ-like in character and in 1898 Max Reger rewrote it for voice and organ. Both the original and later versions are included in this collection. Piano part provided on page 160 (Appendix).

Source: H. Wolf, *Geistliche Lieder*, arranged for single voice and organ by Max Reger, Edition Peters No. 3231. – English version of the text by John Bernhoff (19th century).

Alphabetisches Verzeichnis / Alphabetical Index

Titel und *Textanfänge* / Titles and *Text Incipits*